THE BISHOP'S BONFIRE

THE MACMILLAN COMPANY
NEW YORK · CHICAGO
DALLAS · ATLANTA · SAN FRANCISCO
LONDON · MANILA

SEAN O'CASEY
from a portrait by Breon O'Casey

THE BISHOP'S BONFIRE

BONFIRE

A Sad Play within the Tune of a Polka

BY

SEAN O'CASEY

Cad dhéanfamaoid feasta gan adhmad,
Atá deire na g-coillte ar lár.

New York
THE MACMILLAN COMPANY
1955

TO SUSAN GONE
AND SUSAN HERE

The Bishop's Bonfire was first produced at the Gaiety Theatre, Dublin, on February 28, 1955, with the following cast :

DICK CARRANAUN	Seamus Kavanagh
RICHARD RANKIN	Tony Quinn
COUNCILLOR REILIGAN	Eddie Byrne
VERY REV. TIMOTHY CANON BURREN	Paul Farrell
MANUS MOANROE	Denis Brennan
DANIEL CLOONCOOHY	Aiden Kerrigan
KEELIN	Maureen Cusack
CODGER SLEEHAUN	Cyril Cusack
FR. BOHEROE	Patrick Leyde
FOORAWN	Sheila Brennan
LIEUTENANT MICHAEL REILIGAN	Godfrey Quigley
A RAILWAY PORTER	Harry Hutchinson

The Play was directed by Tyrone Guthrie

CHARACTERS IN THE PLAY

DICK CARRANAUN (*known as the Prodical*), *a mason*

RICHARD RANKIN, *another mason*

COUNCILLOR REILIGAN

VERY REV. TIMOTHY CANON BURREN

MANUS MOANROE

DANIEL CLOONCOOHY

KEELIN, *Councillor Reiligan's daughter*

CODGER SLEEHAUN

FR. BOHEROE, *a curate*

FOORAWN, *Councillor Reiligan's other daughter*

LIEUTENANT MICHAEL REILIGAN, *Councillor Reiligan's son*

A RAILWAY PORTER

———

ACT I.—Councillor Reiligan's house — outside window of drawing-room. Time — about 6 P.M. on an autumn evening.

ACT II.—The drawing-room of Councillor Reiligan's house. Time — later the same evening.

ACT III.—The same. Time — still later.

Act I

The garden of Councillor Reiligan's house. It is not a grand garden, but it is undergoing improvements. A red brick wall is being built at the back. At present it goes two-thirds of the way across the garden, part of it passing behind the house opposite, which is to the right. The finished part has a wrought-iron gate in its centre. To the left the remainder of it is being built, and is only half-way up to where the coping will be when it is finished. A platform runs along this part on which the masons stand while laying a string-course to lift it higher. A few plants, a desperate aspect on them, have been planted along by where the wall has been built. Near the garden's centre is a portly, metal garden urn, moulded into twists and twines, set on a pedestal of new yellow brick. It stands pompously on its pedestal, though looking a little embarrassed that its one use is only to stand and not to serve. Behind the urn is a pile of bricks waiting to be moulded into the part of the wall the masons are building. To the left of the bricks is a rough bench on which a sack of cement stands. A little apart from the urn is a wheelbarrow with a long-handled shovel thrust into it, the blade resting in the barrow, the handle stretched out over the wider end of the barrow. The part of the house seen juts out from the right, crosses the garden diagonally, and mostly consists of a large semi-bow window opening on to the garden. Branches of an ash tree spread out between the end of the house and the wall passing behind it, and under it can be seen, or partly seen, a garden-chair with a gaily coloured canvas, back and seat. Behind the wall, and through the iron gate, the fields and meadows belonging to Reiligan stretch out to the view, and, beyond them, the skyline of the

1

town's buildings, the highest of them, the church spire, thrusts itself up, looking like a stony stork rising from a fleecy nest of cloud. It is a warm, sunny day in the beginning of autumn, when nature gives a last rally and sings a song of colour before winter brings death to flower and field.

Dick Carranaun— known as Prodical— and Richard Rankin are standing on the scaffold, each with a trowel in a right hand which they, alternately, rattle and scrape over the surface of the wall's top. Rankin is a man of about forty, long and lanky, a little bent at the knees, much more apparent when he is walking. His cheeks are reddish-brown, his head bald (he is now wearing a bowler hat, once black, but now turning green, and with its brim frayed by years and use) except for a mousy tuft over either ear and a faint ridge of the same hair at the base of the skull. He wears dark tweed trousers, stained with cement, brown waistcoat, and dark-blue shirt, fading now into a lighter blue colour. His eyebrows are so pale that they are visible only when one is close to him, consequently, when his hat is off, his face and head look somewhat like a bony skull in which the brown eyes still burn, for he is what is known as a 'voteen', one somewhat obsessed with a sense of ever-present sin, and his nostrils frequently sniff the fogs of hell. He neither drinks nor smokes, and his one interest in women is to keep as far away from them as possible. He chooses rather to pray than to whistle when at work. He has the high, falsetto voice of a man unmade.

Prodical is long and lanky too, but whereas Rankin's face is woeful and sour, the Prodical's is sour and pugnacious. He, too, becomes pregnant with a sense of sin after coming out of a drinking-bout, and, at times, when he is in the centre of it. He is always deciding to give up drink altogether, but — in spite of numerous pledges — never quite succeeds. A thick, iron-grey moustache straddles his upper lip. He wears a blue dungaree over his trousers, a patterned cotton shirt, and dirty red braces keep his under trousers in a safe position. His iron-grey hair,

*bushy and uncombed, is protected by a bowler hat of fading
brown, and, as the day is hot, he at times takes this off to wipe
his forehead and the beading sweat from the rim of the hat. Both
masons wear common heavy boots, stained with mortar.*

Rankin [*dolefully*]. Daniel's gone long enough to have
loaded a dozen waggons of hay since. He's stoppin'
away a long time.

Prodical [*indifferently*]. He can stop away for ever, if he
likes, far as I care. [*Rankin is silent.*] An' you want the
job to end so's to get away from me, eh? [*Rankin is
silent.*] Clamin' to be on your own. You can't abide
to be near a decent, God-fearin' mortal whose one
failin' is an occasional drink. [*Rankin is silent.*] Not
a word outa him! I try desperate to keep from it,
but the strain's too much at times. [*Loudly*] You
wouldn't want me to suddenly shoot asunder, would
you? [*Wiping his forehead on the inner rim of his hat*]
We couldn't idle on a better day. [*A pause.*] I
haven't let a drop pass me lip these three days. I try
desperate. [*Loudly*] You wouldn't like to see me
burstin' asunder, would you? Have you no pity?

Rankin. I am what I am.
    [*Councillor Reiligan appears at the window, opens it, and
    allows the Very Reverend Timothy Canon Burren, Parish
    Priest of Ballyoonagh, to step out into the garden. The
    Councillor follows him. There is a great scraping of
    trowels over the wall by the masons. The Canon is a
    short man, below middle height, plump, and a little
    awkwardly built. His legs are short so that he seems to
    trot when he walks. The upper part of his head is
    perfectly round, but the jaws are rather coarsely square-
    set. His face is ruddy and deep lines flow from either*

wing of his nose to the curves of his lower lips ; his upper lip is deep and protruding. His clothes seem to be ill-fitting ; coat a little too big, the trousers coming down only a little below his boot-uppers. The two things about him that are spick and span are his collar and the canonical flash of purple under his chin. He wears a soft black hat, and carries an untidy-looking umbrella.

[Councillor Reiligan is a short man, less than medium height, stocky and sturdy, now developing an imposing paunch. His face is ruddy, weather-beaten, and wrinkled, looking older than his fifty-five years. He has small, piercing, pig-like eyes, and his chin and neck are hidden by a red beard, now turning grey. Reddish hair on his head has receded from the front so that the front half of his head is bald. He is dressed in morning clothes, frock coat, striped trousers, all a little too baggy for him, except that part of his clothing enclosing his waist. He is the biggest money-man in the district, a loyal pillar of the clergy, and has a great power and influence in the affairs of the state — the local member of the Dail could never climb into a seat without the backing of Councillor Reiligan. He carries in his hand a silk tall-hat which he puts on when he enters the garden.

Canon [with finality]. Manus Moanroe is not a person to have about the place, Councillor. I've said so before. You should remember he had an eye on your Foorawn before he became a seminarist and before she entered the convent. You know the scamp he has become since he flung his vocation away, and since he served in the English air force.

Reiligan [apologetically]. I know, I know : an unfortunate poor man. Maybe, Canon, there's not much harm in him. He's been a godsend to me. With his checkin'

things comin' in and things goin' out, and his wary
way of keepin' me accounts, he musta saved me more'n
half a thousand pounds.

Canon. You think too much of mere money-making,
Councillor. I must remind you that there are more
important things than even half a thousand pounds.

Reiligan [meekly]. I know, Canon ; sure, I know that ;
though Father Boheroe thinks something of Manus.

Canon [with cold anger]. I am Parish Priest of Ballyoonagh,
Reiligan !

Reiligan [meekly]. Sure, I know, Canon. I know. [To
escape, he turns on the masons.] What are the two of
yous doin', standin' there motionless like gorged gulls
airin' themselves on a quay-wall ? Yous know the
church tower has to be built well as the wall.

Rankin [in his high, falsetto voice]. We're waitin' for Daniel
to bring us the bricks.

Prodical [in his deep baritone]. Waitin' for Daniel to bring
us the mortar.

Reiligan [mimicking them in turn]. Waitin' for Daniel to
bring us the bricks ; waitin' for him to bring us the
mortar. [Furiously] Hop off the platform an' get them
yourselves !

Rankin. Masons is supposed to have the things brought
to them.

Prodical. That's a labourer's job.

Canon [to Rankin]. We're all labourers, Rankin. When
you are working for the Councillor, Rankin, however
menial the job may be, you are serving God. We

want you masons for the church tower ; so get a move on.

Rankin [*jumping down and running to the bricks*]. Yis, Canon.

Reiligan [*looking at his gold watch*]. We better be goin', Canon, if we're to be in time to meet Monsignor Mulligan. [*As they go towards the gate*] The wall'll look fine when it's finished. When it is, I'm goin' to have it covered with climbin' roses.

Canon [*petulantly*]. Roses ? Pshaw ! What put such a useless idea into your head ? Ballyoonagh hasn't the time to go wading through roses. Roses cost money, Councillor. The church needs money more than your wall needs roses !

Reiligan. I know, I know, Canon ; I only thought a rose here an' there might do no harm.

Canon. They mightn't and they might. They might provoke envy. Put nodding roses in this garden, and it wouldn't be long till others wanted nodding roses in theirs. I don't want the needs of our church to lie hidden in the petals of a rose.

Reiligan. I know, Canon, I know. I like roses, tho' I don't know why : a foolish wish, Canon, right enough ; but somehow, I always longed for a rose to lie in me Sunday coat.
    [*They go out by the gate, and pass by behind the wall, only their heads and shoulders showing.*

Canon [*as they pass on behind the wall*]. The coat's better without one. The wall itself, even, wasn't really needed. You'll have to guard yourself, Michael,

against pride and vanity.   Your wall will do fine
without your roses.   Roses indeed !

[*They pass out on path behind the wall, the Canon leading
the way, commenting on the roses ; the Councillor meekly
following.*]

Rankin [*indignantly*]. Roses indeed !   We all know what
happened before in a beautiful garden among the roses.
Can't he plant ivy ?   It grows quicker, looks as well,
costs nothin', an' sinful love can't quicken in it.   Roses
indeed !   Our Blessed Lady's rose enough for Ballyoonagh.

Prodical [*contemptuously*]. Roses !   Maybe it's roses he
wants !   Isn't he stuck-up enough without a rose
gildin' a coat !   I always liked a rose, says he.   Goin'
about himself like a blasted bonnie bunch of roses o !
The Canon soon put an end to his dream.

[*He takes up a brick from those that Rankin has carried to
the platform, and goes to lay it.*]

Rankin [*whipping it from the Prodical, and laying it on his end of
the wall*].   Eh, there, that's mine.   Get your own bricks.

Prodical [*indignantly — as Rankin is bedding it*]. You're a
nice christian cut-throat, denyin' a buttie a few
bricks !   [*Admonitorily*] Remember what your Canon
said that when you served oul' Reiligan, you served
God ; so as I'm servin' Reiligan, by servin' me, you're
servin' God, too.   [*He snatches the brick back angrily and
starts to set it in his own part of the wall.*] Good catholic
an' all as you call yourself, you're not goin' to be let
bounce yourself into an authority you've no legal or
christian right to !   I'll not be bounced.

Rankin [*indignantly*]. It's you's a bouncer, but I'm not

goin' to stand you bouncin' away the bricks I carried over for meself ! I'll not be bounced either !

[*Prodical has tapped the brick home with the tip of the handle of his trowel, and now goes to take another brick from those beside Rankin ; but Rankin pushes him away so that he has to jump down from the scaffolding. Rankin then takes the brick Prodical has set, and starts to bed it in his own part of the wall.*

Prodical [*angrily getting back on to the scaffold and sending Rankin off it with an angry push*]. Mind who you're pushin' ! You're exhibitin' a nice kind of catholic conduct.

Rankin [*getting back on to the scaffold*]. I am what I am, but you'll not lord it over me. It's my brick — I carried it.

Prodical. It's not your brick an' it's not my brick ; it's nobody's brick ; if it's anybody's brick, it's God's brick.

Rankin [*gripping Prodical by an arm and reaching for the brick which Prodical holds behind his back*]. It's mine rightfully. It's in my charge for the moment. Gimme it.

Prodical [*trying to pull his arm free*]. It'll do you good to be denied. The brick hasn't been designated to you. Let go !

Rankin. You let go ! It hasn't been designated to you either. Let go !

Prodical. I won't let go !

Rankin. You'll have to let go !

[*Rankin pulls Prodical to the left, Prodical pulls Rankin back to the right, their struggle bringing them to the edge of the scaffold, till one of the struggles forces them to jump off the scaffolding together.*

[*Manus has come in, and is seen behind the wall.   He enters the garden by the gate, goes over to the barrow, sits down on a handle, and watches the couple disputing.   He has a note-book and pencil in his hand.   Manus Moanroe is thirty or so, tall and well built.   He looks slovenly now, with a beard of a week's growth, and a face lined more than his years warrant, warped by a sad and sullen look.   He is wearing old air-force trousers, frayed at the bottoms, coarse boots beginning to go at the toes ; his cotton shirt is soiled, and one torn sleeve but comes to the elbow.   At the moment he is wearing neither waistcoat nor coat, though an old grey felt hat covers his head, its flabby brim pulled down over his eyes.*

[*Prodical and Rankin stand bunched together as if they were about to begin a bout of wrestling, one angry face glaring at the other equally angry one.*

Prodical [*gripping Rankin by the shoulders and shaking him*]. I'll wrastle you if you want to wrastle !   I'll bring back your catholic conscience, you holy hoodlum, muckin' me about like you were on a prairie outa sight of God an' scholarship !

Rankin [*now shaking the Prodical who has grown tired of shaking Rankin, and is now panting*]. Call me what you like, but say nothin' against me religion !   [*In a squeal*] 'Gainst me religion, see !

[*Though gripping themselves in the manner of wrestling, the two boyos content themselves with shoving each other to and fro in a semi-rhythmic movement to the accompaniment of their arguments, Manus, from his seat on the barrow, conducting the movements with mock gestures.*

Prodical [*vehemently*]. True religion isn't puffed up, you bastard ; it's long-sufferin' an' kind, an' never vaunts itself like you do ; true religion doesn't envy a man a brick, you rarefied bummer !

Manus [*angry and exasperated — flinging his note-book at them*]. Give over your fightin' for bricks of clay, the way Reiligan fights for the gold ones, you god-frightened fools ! [*He gets up, and pushes them asunder.*] You spoilers of men's hopes and men's fancies ; you curses on Ballyoonagh where the rust of hell is on everything that's done there.

Prodical [*indignantly — retreating to the scaffolding*]. What're you ? Who are you to talk ? You didn't do much for yourself. A dirty leaf torn out of a book. A labourer, no more, now. Now you're here, you bring us the mortar and the bricks we need.

Manus [*picking up his note-book, and returning to the barrow — wearily*]. Oh, go to hell !

Prodical. You'd better do it. When we're done here, we're wanted to work on the church tower, and the Canon's in a hurry. He said so.

Rankin [*sharp and strong falsetto*]. The Canon said so.

Manus. And God stops talking to listen when the Canon speaks. Aw, go to hell, and carry the Canon along with you ; [*fiercely*] on your backs takin' turns with the carrying, bring yourselves to hell, and bear the Canon with you !
  [*Daniel Clooncoohy is seen coming behind the wall. He opens the gate, and enters the garden. He is young, twenty-five or so, and good-looking in a rugged way. His face is open and innocent, though sometimes shadowed with a furtive look ; neither sure of himself nor sure of his future. He wears flannel trousers, tweed waistcoat,*

*and carries an old grey coat over an arm. When he is in
the garden, he drapes the coat over the wall, and goes to
the barrow, sits down on it, opposite side to Manus, takes
out a cigarette, lights it, and begins to smoke.*

Prodical [*to Daniel*]. Come on, Daniel, more bricks ;
hurry up ! Attaboy ! You couldn't have been that
long tumblin' hay. We have a wall to build, lad ; a
duty to do.

Rankin. More mortar, Daniel ; come on, hurry up ! We
have our consciences to mind.

Daniel [*to Manus, ignoring the call — intensely and delightedly*].
The Codger has discovered a keg, Manus — a beauty !
The wood was swellin' with the soaked-in juice left
behind. He's drenched it gently with more'n half a
gallon of boilin' water, an' left it to mature in the sun.
I've tasted it, an' it's like the fire of love meltin' into
dew.

Manus. I know. I found the keg. He's bringing it here.

Prodical [*impatiently*]. Come on, Dan ; more bricks here.
We have to hurry. We have to get goin' on the
church tower.

Rankin. Canon said so.

Prodical. Some bricks, Dan. When we're done here,
we've got to tackle the church tower.

Rankin. More mortar, Daniel. Here today ; church
tower tomorrow. The Canon said so.

Manus [*to Daniel*]. Go on, Dan. [*He rises from sitting on
the barrow.*] We have to keep building our temples
higher and higher till the shouting of heavenly pride
encases and hides the growling-grumble of men. The

church tower, Dan ; the church tower ! [*He pushes Dan to the bricks.*] Go on ! God is waiting. He mustn't be made to stand in a queue. [*Daniel takes the barrow and trundles it under the ash tree round to the back of the house. Manus looks at the pile of bricks, and glances at the bag of cement. Jotting down a few figures*] Another thousand bricks should do the job, and with the cement at the back, this bag here'll be enough.

> [*Daniel returns to the farther end of the scaffolding with mortar in the barrow. He shovels some of it on to the mortar-board that lies between the masons ; then shoves the barrow away to where it had been before.*

Prodical [*calling to where Daniel has gone*]. Bricks now, Dan.

Rankin [*calling as Prodical did*]. More bricks, Dan.

> [*Daniel comes back, goes over to the bricks, and is about to collect them for the masons, when Keelin appears at the window, and beckons him. Keelin is a handsome lass of twenty-five. Her hair is a ripe auburn, more red than brown, and it surrounds her head in great fuzzy clusters, standing out from it so that it looks like a burning bush. Her figure is slim, though her breasts be buxom. She is dressed in a dark-green skirt, reaching just to her knees, a white blouse, amber nylon stockings, black shoes, and a lighter green apron, trimmed with dark red, protects her skirt and the front of her blouse from damage during housework.*

Keelin [*beckoning to Daniel — lovingly and softly*]. Come on in, Dan. They want your help to shift a wardrobe in a bedroom.

> [*Daniel runs over and hurries into the house by the window. Keelin blows a kiss to Manus, a gracious kiss.*

Rankin [*working last brick on scaffold into wall*]. Last brick goin' in, Dan. More bricks, more bricks.

Keelin [*in a loud, sharp, and authoritative voice*]. Richard Rankin !

Rankin [*wheeling round to face her at the sound of authority*]. Yis, Miss Keelin ?

Keelin [*roguishly lifting her skirt to above her knees*]. How do you like my nylons, darling ?

Rankin [*with an hysterical moan of shame-filled anguish*]. Ooh no ; [*he wheels convulsively to turn his back to her.*] I didn't look, I didn't see !

Keelin. Yes, you did.

Rankin. No, I didn't.

Manus [*to Keelin*]. The nylons aren't as handsome as the legs, Keelin.

Rankin [*revolving round to look at her again*]. I was taken unawares, I was. [*He revolves agitatedly to face away from her.*] So I was, I was. [*He revolves to look at her again— almost shouting.*] I won't look, I won't, I won't ! [*He revolves again till he is facing away.*] Shoo her away, men. [*In a faint voice*] Oh, do, please ! [*Exhausted, he half leans, half lies over the wall.*] I'm dizzy, I'm dazzled !

Prodical. God, man, take it easy ! [*Shaking him*] You're not goin' to die.

Manus [*with animation — to Keelin*]. That was a sudden sight to make a young heart thrill thinking of things to come, and an old heart tremble thinking of things gone by !
  [*Keelin bows to Manus, blows him another kiss, points at Rankin, and goes in again, leaving the window ajar.*

Prodical [*glancing round garden, and seeing no Daniel*]. God damn it — where's that bastard, Dan, gone to now !

Manus [*bitterly*]. Gone into the house and into hell, where his one aching desire will be to get Keelin into his arms, and her one desire to find herself there ; but nothing will come to them save, maybe, an accidental touching of hands.

Prodical [*mocking*]. Them two'll never kiss in front of the Councillor's face or behind his back either. [*Down to Manus*] Keelin's reckoned a lady, an' the moon will never shine on them two with their heads too close together.

Manus [*fiercely*]. Shut up, you two wizened wisps of dust ! You shadows of coming events to Daniel and to me ! [*He sits dejectedly on the barrow's handles, musingly.*] Keelin, Foorawn, Daniel, me, you are on the swift way to become but dusty questions that life has never answered. No frond of a child's laugh shall ever spring from us.

Prodical [*down to him — scornfully*]. Have sense, man ! Isn't it the laugh of the town an' district, him loungin' after Keelin, an' you loungin' after Foorawn ?

Manus [*fiercely*]. Shut up, I say, you neon light of ignorance and ruin ! Oh, Foorawn, Foorawn, time shall toss wrinkles on to your sweet face, shall wither your breasts, shall bring your knees to a bending ; but no bonny breeze of life shall ever blow your skirt aside.

Prodical [*down to Manus*]. If it's all the same to you, Manus, we want no double-meanin' talk here.

Manus. Oh, listen to them, look at them. Two of the people of God's hand, two sheep of his pasture ! Away, you slimy touch of hell !

Prodical [*in a semi-shout*]. We believe in God, an' you don't !

[*Rankin has got down from scaffold and has gone over to the window.*

Rankin [*at the window, calling plaintively into the room*]. Daniel, Daniel !

Manus. I don't know which of you's the bigger bum — him who thinks he's given to heaven, or you who know you're given to drink.

Prodical [*getting off the scaffold and going to Rankin by the window — loudly and defiantly as he goes*]. I believe in God, an' you don't. [*Prodding Rankin's arm*] Eh, Dick ? We believe in God, an' he doesn't, don't we ?

Rankin [*plaintively*]. I don't want to be entered into the talk. He is what he is ; you are what you are ; I am what I am. I don't want to be led into a tangle of talk.

Prodical [*indignantly*]. Are you afraid to stand up for your religion, or wha' ? We believe in God, an' he doesn't, don't we ?

Rankin [*with a plaintive yelp*]. Yis ! [*Plaintively calling into the room*] Daniel, Daniel !

Prodical [*impatiently*]. Damn it, man, a mouse wouldn't hear that call. Put some force into it, an' make it reverabate through the house. [*Shouting*] Daniel !

Rankin [*just as plaintively as before*]. Daniel !

Prodical [*shouting*]. Daniel ! Damn you, are you comin' ? [*To Rankin*] Call out together — loud ! Now !

Prodical [*loudly*]
Rankin [*plaintively*] } [*together*]. Daniel !

[*Manus, who has been risen from the barrow, and has gone to the left to watch westwards, now meets the Codger coming in gloriously with a keg on his left shoulder.*

[*He is heard singing before he is seen, and continues when he appears.*

Codger (*singing*) :
  Ah, them were the days when th' sickles were keen,
  Th' barley bright yellow, the grass a rich green ;
  When our feet beat th' road on th' way to cut corn,
  An' the dew turn'd the world to a diamond-clad morn.

  [*The Codger is eighty-four years old ; but carries his age about with him in a jaunty and defiant way. He is tall, thin, and wiry, his face deeply seamed with many wrinkles from weathers and old age, and is strongly tanned, and as tough as leather. His head is covered with a crisp, thick mop of white hair, his upper-lip hidden by a white moustache, and his chin by a shovel-shaped white beard ; his dark eyes are alert and sparkling. He wears old black trousers, caught up and held in place by a leather belt ornamented and heavy with many brass badges of British regiments, a gaily chequered cotton shirt, without a waistcoat, and his white hair is half covered by an old, soiled, grey trilby hat. His old brown coat is slung over his right arm, and his right hand holds the shaft of a hay-fork which he is trailing behind him.*
  [*As he is crossing, Daniel comes hurrying out of the house by the window, shoving aside Rankin and the Prodical, his eyes fixed on the keg the Codger is carrying.*

Daniel [*shoving Rankin and Prodical aside*]. Mind your-selves ; get outa the way.

Prodical [*seeing the keg*]. Ah, me sowl man, Codger !

Daniel [*running in front of Codger*]. Come on, me sowl man
— we'll dump it behind the laurels.
   [*He goes off past the ash tree. Rankin and the Prodical go
   back to the scaffold, get up on it, Rankin scraping wall
   with his trowel, the Prodical fascinated by the keg.
   Manus goes along with the Codger, who halts beside the
   ash tree, and looks at it.*

Codger [*gazing at the tree*]. The ash is beginnin' to shed its
leaves already. Odd, how the old leaves drop so early
an' the young ones come so late.

Manus [*quoting*]. Delaying as the tender ash delays
To clothe herself when all the woods are green.

Codger [*fervently*]. Yet I love it ; love it better than the
beech herself.

Manus. The ash, Codger, gave the wood for the shafts for
the spears of the ancient Greeks, and for the pikes we
used ourselves to free Ireland through the sad year of
Ninety-eight.

Daniel [*appearing round the tree — impatiently*]. What the
hell's keepin' yous ? Come on, Codger, with the keg.
   [*The Codger goes on round the tree, followed by Manus.
   Prodical is looking longingly after them. He gets down
   from the scaffold, is about to follow, but climbs back
   again, and keeps looking towards where they have gone.
   Rankin is busy scraping the top of the wall, with one eye
   watching the Prodical.*

Rankin [*persuasively*]. Be careful, man. Look the other
way, Prodical. Have a little spiritual spunk, an' act
as if the gin-keg wasn't there.

Prodical [*firmly*]. It is there, isn't it ? I didn't call the
keg into being, did I ? I haven't the power to conjure

the keg into bodiless existence, have I? I can't work miracles, can I? Your likes or dislikes isn't goin' to control the progress of the world. The keg's here now, an' can't be avoided, can it? We'll have to suffer it, like it, or dislike it.

Rankin. There's the church tower to think of, too.

Prodical. That's a perspective contingency ; a *primae facie*. That other subject's a factuality of here and now.

Rankin. You said a short time ago that it was goin' to be never again with you.

Prodical [*protestingly*]. I'm not to blame for you over-hearin' silent things. What I murmured was sotto vossie. I'm not a factotum to me own whisperin's into me own ear.

Rankin. It wasn't said sotto vossie. It was outspoken, an' next door to a vow.

Prodical [*indignantly*]. It was no vow ! It had no habili-ments of any vow on it. It was a *sub rosa* understandin' or misunderstandin' with meself.

Rankin [*plaintively to Prodical*]. Your good angel's trying to pull you back, Prodical ; but if you once get to the keg, you're cornered ! It's an occasion of sin, an' may do immortal harm to your poor soul !

Prodical [*coming over to Rankin and thrusting his face upwards towards Rankin — indignantly*]. Looka, me good angel, I won't have you hoverin' over me soul like a saygull over a fish too deep for a dive down ! I'm not goin' to let foreign bodies write down messages on me soul the way a body writes down things on a Christmas card. [*Preparing to jump from the scaffold*] Me soul's me own particular compendium.   Me soul's me own spiritual property, complete an' entire, verbatim in all its concernment.

> [*He jumps down to the ground, and goes to the tree.*

Rankin [*calling after him*]. If you'd only listen, you'd hear your good angel callin' you back from the keg !

Prodical [*halting and turning round — annoyed at being checked*]. What's it to an angel if I go calmly after a keg ?   What's it to an angel if I trot after a keg ?   [*He returns swiftly to the edge of the scaffold, and glares angrily at Rankin.*]   What is it to the angel if I go at a gallop after a keg ?

Rankin [*his back turned to Prodical*]. Aha, you're waverin'. You're half afraid.   I hear the shakin' in your voice.

Prodical [*beside himself with rage*]. You buttoned-up delusion, there's ne'er a quiver in me voice !   It's dense with concentration, but it's under calm control.

Rankin.   Listen to your good angel's warnin' !

Prodical [*loudly*]. How the hell d'ye know what me own angel's thinkin' ?   How d'ye know me own good angel isn't smilin' ?   How d'ye know me own angel doesn't know what I do or don't do is me fate ?

> [*He goes again towards the tree.*

Rankin [*firmly — turning to shout after the Prodical*]. My angel's tellin' me to urge you to listen to your own angel's warning !

Prodical [*shouting back from where he stands at the tree*]. I'm not goin' to have your angel interferin' with my angel ! A keg here, or a keg there, is no proper positive subject for an angel to bother about.

Rankin [*positively*]. Like it or no, your good angel's at your elbow drawin' you back from the curse in the keg !

Prodical [*in a wild shout*]. Listen you an' listen all ! I don't want, an' I'm not goin' to have, an angel always be me side to tap me on the shoulder every time I stir ! Tap tap tap !
> [*He makes off around the ash tree, after the keg. Rankin stands silent on the scaffolding for a few moments ; then he takes off his hat, and indulges in a prayer ; after the prayer, he gets down to the ground, goes over to the bricks, carries some of them over to the scaffold, comes back to them, pauses, takes off his hat again, and begins to pray. Keelin comes to the window, looks out and around the garden.*]

Keelin [*to Rankin*]. Where's Dan ? [*He takes no notice, but continues to pray. She watches Rankin for a moment, and then goes softly over to him.*] Sweet man, d'ye never get tired prayin' ? [*He is startled, slides his hat back on to his head, but keeps his back turned to her.*] You know, Mr. Rankin, too much of a good thing may be bad for a man, while a little of a bad thing may be good for him.

Rankin [*resentful*]. God knows what is good for me.

Keelin [*coaxingly*]. Don't be so sure : what you think God is thinkin' may be only your own thinkin' formed in your own mind to satisfy and please yourself. The other day, Foorawn said what you said to Father Boheroe, but he laughed, laughed at her. The priest laughed. D'ye know what he said ?

Rankin [*going at a jog-trot to the ash tree, halting there, cupping his hands over his mouth, and calling*]. Daniel !

Keelin [*following and standing behind him*]. Father Boheroe said that a man learns what's good for him by experience ; an', often, a woman as well as God knew what was good for a man. So there !

Rankin [*doing a jog-trot back to the bricks, and lifting some to the scaffold*]. I haven't time to talk ; I have to get on with me work.

Keelin [*following him*]. How d'ye know God lets you know what He believes is good for you, anyhow ?

Rankin [*confused and embarrassed*]. You should know yourself — be mortification, prayer, and what the priest says.

Keelin [*mocking*]. What about Father Boheroe then ? He told me once that what a priest says to a layman isn't always evidence. He said too that a lot of what crawthumpers like you tell us God said to them is nothin' but a conceited an' ignorant mind blatherin' to itself. Think of that !

Rankin [*suddenly, stiff-standing, suspicious — vehemently*]. I don't want to think of it ! [*Slyly*] You seem to do a lot of talkin' with Father Boheroe.

Keelin [*cautiously*]. I do some talkin' as you do yourself. What about it ?

Rankin [*slyly with a touch of malice*]. Doesn't sound proper for a priest to talk too much to a good-lookin' girl. I seen a young swalla this mornin'. Flyin' swift he was like he was carousin' close to heaven.

Keelin [*hilariously*]. Now you do a carousin' close to earth, fancy boy. Never mind the flying swalla — there's a far prettier birdie standin' beside you now. It's

nice to know Father Boheroe thinks me good-lookin',
an' nicer, darling, when you look at me, you think so
too.

Rankin [*head bent lower still*]. I didn't look at you, I don't
look at you. The swalla musta been a young one ;
alone there, up so high, dancin' like in a wide, wide
space of blue light.

Keelin [*teasingly*]. Look at me, now, an' never mind the
swalla. You must have looked at me to know I'm
good-lookin'.

Rankin. I never looked ; not the way I looked at the
swalla. The knowin' about it came out in the talk I
heard from others. I never looked ; only at the swalla
up high away from man in a wide world of his own.

Keelin. You're just tryin' to be shy, dear. Now's your
time to have a long ravishin' look at me. [*She slips
round to face him.*] Look at me the way you looked
at the dancin' swalla.

Rankin [*swiftly turning his back to her — confused*]. Your Da
wants to put roses along the wall. Roses along the wall,
the wall. Can't he put ivy there instead ? Looks as
well ; costs nothin'.

Keelin. Yes, yes, ivy would be grand, an' then, like the
ivy, I'd cling to thee !

Rankin [*agitated and confused*]. Yis, yis ; no, no, no ! The
wall. Oh, go away, Miss. [*With as loud a shout as he is
capable of*] Daniel !

Keelin [*reproachfully*]. Now, don't be so rude as to turn
your back on a good-looking lady. Here, do something to keep you from the sin of idleness. [*She slips*

*round to face him, pulls up her skirt as far as her knee, and
shows a trim leg in a nylon stocking.*] Stoop down and tie
my shoe-lace tighter, and mind you, no naughty tricks !
Look, and let yourself live for a minute !

[*Rankin gives a shuddering, frightened start when he sees
the nyloned leg, jerks his head up from the sight, looks
Keelin in the eyes for a second, then viciously spits in
her smiling face. Surprised and startled, she jumps back,
searching frantically in a pocket for a handkerchief.
Rankin hurries away to the scaffold, jumps up on it, picks
up his trowel, plunges it into the mortar remaining on
the mortar-board, and appears to be very busy.*

Keelin [*violently wiping her face with her handkerchief*]. You
dirty, evil-minded lugworm ! You huckster of hollow
an' spiteful holiness ! You get ! [*She hurries to the
window, turning when she gets there, to throw a few more
angry words at him.*] Looka the fella who wants to be
great with God ! Christ, you'll make a commotion
when you get, you get, to where you're goin' ! Crawlin'
to heaven the way the snake crawled outa Eden !
Damn you, you God's remorse for men !

Rankin [*almost wailing*]. Daniel ! [*To Keelin*] I'll tell the
Canon all you said, me lassie.

Keelin [*furiously*]. Tell the Bishop, you canting cod ; tell
the Pope, you blob of dung !
[*She goes into the house by the window, closing it angrily
after her.*
[*After a pause through which Rankin works at the wall,
Father Boheroe saunters in by the path behind the wall.
When he comes in by the gate, we see that he is in his
early thirties, and of middle height. His clerical clothes
are old and beginning to fade, with creases in coat, vest,*

and trousers ; only the white collar is without one. His face is a rugged one, surmounted by a thoughtful, wrinkled brow ; but his eyes are bright, searching at times, but often somewhat sad and thoughtful ; though they are not incapable of a roguish twinkle or two when he sees or hears some foolish thing said or done by some foolish mortal. His boots are strong ones, dusty and somewhat muddy with much walking. He wears no hat, but his dark and bushy hair protects his head well from rain or sun. A man of the world as well as a man of God. He strolls over to where Rankin is working.

Father Boheroe. Good day, mason.

Rankin [*whipping off his hat*]. Good day, Father.

Father Boheroe. Put your hat on. It's warm today. Where are your butties ?

Rankin [*righteously*]. I'm sorry to say, Father, that they're all gathered round a keg, among the laurels, drinking.

Father Boheroe [*brightly*]. Ah, trying to get a glimpse of heaven through the wrong window. We often do that, too, through false piety, or through foolish sin. So that was why I heard Keelin shouting as I came along — urging them to come back to their work ?

Rankin. I wasn't listenin' ; I thought I heard a voice. I was busy thinkin' only of the work I was doin'.

Father Boheroe. The work ; ah yes, the work. Never-ending work, yet few fruits come from it. [*Musing*] Just a little life. No colour, no thought ; lean cattle, thin milk ; worn-out meadows giving dusty hay ; not a single building calling a halt for a look at it ; not even the tawdry church.

Rankin [*shocked*]. The church, Father? Oh, Father, the church. I'd be afraid to say anything against a sacred place.

Father Boheroe [*impatiently*]. All places are sacred, man; the church we pray in, the homes sheltering us, the shops where we get the things we need to go on living, the halls we dance in; yea, the very place we walk on is holy ground. Work, too, is holy, but only when it's reasonable. Work, Rankin, can bless, but it can blast, too, as it is blasting little Keelin, who should be living with a gay young lad in a house of her own.

Rankin. Keelin, is it? Anyone here'll tell you, Father, there's ne'er a man in Ballyoonagh fit to marry into the family.

Father Boheroe. They say that, do they? An' what does God say, I wonder?

Rankin [*frightened*]. I dunno. [*He moves to part of platform nearest to ash tree — calling*] Daniel! [*To Father Boheroe*] Ballyoonagh's holy, Father, an' we have to put down anything that doesn't fit into what we know God doesn't like.

Father Boheroe [*suddenly catching hold of Rankin as if he were frightened*]. Whisht! Did you hear that sound of rending?

Rankin [*greatly startled*]. What sound? Oh, what sound of rending, Father?

Father Boheroe. The sounds of clawing hands, of pious fools tearing God's good manners into little pieces!

Rankin [*gasping*]. Sacred Heart, you frightened me! I dunno, I dunno; I was only thinkin' of Keelin an', an', an' of Dan an' of meself.

Father Boheroe. Ay, of Keelin, of Dan, and of yourself. Keelin's a fine girl but works too hard for too little. Too much work misfits a soul for heaven and for here, Rankin. Keelin's a grand girl, an' should have a wide an' merrier corner in life. Too much formal prayer, Rankin, sometimes makes a soul conceited ; and merriment may be a way of worship !

Rankin [*viciously*]. It's mostly merriment with her right enough. It's often said, Father, she does very queer things at times.

Father Boheroe. Is it, now ? Oh, well, it was said of our Blessed Lord that He did very queer things at times. Maybe He did ; maybe she does too. If I only knew her moments of merriment, I'd join her. [*Suddenly — to Rankin*] Are you in love with Keelin by any chance ?

Rankin [*fiercely*]. What, me ? That one ! No, I amn't, I amn't, I amn't ! A one that waits only for the beck of a finger to laurel herself with light livin' ! [*With clenched teeth*] I hate the evil Eves who send men sidling into sin !

> [*Before Father Boheroe can get out of his surprise at Rankin's vehement protests, the Codger appears, returning to the garden by the ash tree. He is trying to walk upright like a guardsman. His eyes have something of a wild light in them, excited rather than drunk, but, all the same, half-lit with diluted gin. He goes towards the heap of bricks, the hay-fork over his shoulder like a gun.*]

Codger [*jovial but dignified*]. Good morrow, good Father ; good morrow again. Rare day. Day for the beatin' of a big drum ! Brrum brrumm ! I'm the sole Sleehawn left standin' here in Ballyoonagh. Wife dead (rest her soul), two daughters an' three sons away, away in

America, leavin' me the one lone, mohican Sleehawn left standin' in Ballyoonagh. Fly away, Peter, fly away, Paul ; fly away, Susan, fly away all — a fly-away country, this of ours, Father ; this country of ours. Man has to set his face to face things, eh, Father ? God's more than a mere melodeon-player. Yis, man has more to do than just sing for his supper. Be rights, I should be helpin' with the hay. Hay, is it ? God ! No heart in the soil, no heart in the grass that tops it. Hay from grass that never had a life. I suppose I shouldn't say these things, Father, to you, anyhow.

Father Boheroe. Why not, Michael, when they're true ? God is unhappy when we don't do what we can with what He gives us.

Codger [*emphatically*]. 'Course He is ! A man's more than a mayfly ; though the dance of the mayflies itself has a midget glory of its own. [*He sits down on the bricks.*] That's what we have now — a midget glory : [*pauses — musingly and liltingly*] slower and slower and slower the wheel swings, lower and lower and lower the reel rings. [*Daniel now comes in marching as the Codger marched in before him. He goes to the bricks, takes up two, goes to scaffold, and dumps them down on it. He returns to the bricks for more, never bending as he marches.*

Codger [*taking out an old pipe, and lighting it.*] Take it easy, Daniel, take it easy.
   [*The Prodical now comes in marching as the two before had done. He goes to mount the scaffold, but though able to balance on two legs, he fails to do it haughtily on one, so he loses his balance, and suddenly grips hold of Rankin, who holds on to the wall, and so the Prodical manages to*

*pull himself up, pull himself together, and, at last, stand
as erect on the platform as he had stood on the ground.*

Prodical [*as he loses balance*]. Woa ! False step. Uups a
daisy ! I feel fine, gentlemen. Men at work, Father.
No finer sight in nature. No, none. [*Shoving Rankin
from him*] Move over, an' let a man get goin'. [*He does
mime movements of a dance.*] You promenade down the
centre an' split the way in two, go through the open
window, an' swing your Sindy Sue !

Daniel [*to Father Boheroe*]. You know, Father, that the
Bishop is comin' to Ballyoonagh ; comin' to his own
home town ; Bill Mullarkey that was ; the one who
older people know as a kid runnin' wild through the
streets of Ballyoonagh.

Father Boheroe [*unimpressed*]. Is he ? Oh, yes ; I remember
the Canon told me about it. A great time coming.

Codger. Faith, Bill Mullarkey'll be handier with a hay-
fork than he'll ever be with a crozier.

Prodical [*to Codger*]. No blasphemin', you. [*To Father
Boheroe*] Manus told us, Father. I feel fine. He's
comin' all right ; comin' in his purple cassock, golden
mitre, an' satin shoon. Nothin' grander — purple an'
gold, with the sheen of satin on them all.

Rankin. A great time coming.

Codger. What are the things that God gives to one man
to the things God gives to all ? What's the gold on
a bishop's mitre to the gold on the gorse ? The sheen
of his satin shoon to the feel of a petal on the wildest
rose ? What's a bishop's purple to the purple in the
silky plume of the speary thistle ?

Prodical. Still an' all, the Bishop'll bring a few golden days to Ballyoonagh.

Codger. Ay, golden days of penance an' prayer [*indicating Rankin*] for God's gaum there ; but not for me. Me golden days is over. [*He chants gaily and a little gloomily :*]
Ah, them were th' golden days with an arm round a waist,
When everything shone so shy an' gay ;
When a man had heart to toss the girls as well as time to toss th' hay—
Oh, them were th' days when life had something fine to say !

Prodical [*warningly*]. Now, now, Codger ! [*To Father Boheroe*] Ay, an' Reiligan has a gang sweatin' mill-streams buildin' a great bonfire to light a welcome to the comin' Bishop, an' piles of bad books an' evil pictures on top of it are to go away in flames.

Rankin [*stuttering with rage*]. Pitch them in, all in — bad pictures, bad books — pitch them into the burnin' bonfire !

Codger. Reiligan ought to pitch his hay into it, too, for there's none of God's growin' in it. [*He rises up from sitting on the bricks.*] Be God, I'll go an' tell him !

Keelin [*appearing at the window*]. Me Da's on the phone, Father. He asked if you were here. I seen you from a window upstairs. He says he has news for you. Will you come in, Father ?

Codger [*to Father Boheroe*]. In with you, Father, an' tell him to do the decent thing be makin' a bonfire of Ballyoonagh, Bishop, books an' all !
[*Father Boheroe crosses over and goes in by the window with Keelin to the house.*

Prodical [*gaily*]. Now then, let's get goin' !   Come on, Dan, loads of brick an' mortar till we cope the wall, an' cry *finis*.

Daniel [*indicating bag of cement on the bench — to the Codger*]. Come on, an' give's a hand to carry this to the barrow.

Codger [*contemptuously*]. Give you a hand !   Didja hear him ?   [*Angrily*] Why, man, when I was your age, I'd carry that between me finger an' me thumb !   Put it on your back, man, an' show you're no cissy.

Daniel [*resentfully*]. You put it on your back, if you're so eager.

Codger. Ay, an' carry it where it's to go, without losin' a breath.

Daniel [*sneering*]. You crazy old fool, you can't even handle your rosary beads without puffin' !

Codger [*shoving Daniel from the sack*]. Get outa th' way ! I'll show you !   [*He turns his back to the sack, and grips it by the lugs.*]   I'll show yous all !

Prodical [*over to the Codger*]. You let that alone, an' go back to your harmless hay !

Codger [*giving the sack a vicious tug on to his back — as he starts on his journey*]. I'll show yous all !

Daniel [*frightened — warningly*]. Steady !   [*Codger starts off at a trot facing towards the window ; the weight is too much for him, and his trot grows into a gallop ; he has to run to save himself from falling on his face.   The others watching him are stupefied, Daniel standing stiffly upright, Prodical bending forwards from the scaffold, his mouth wide open ; Rankin, seeing what is going to happen, turns his back, crosses himself, takes off*

*hat and bends his head in prayer.   Calling after the Codger in
a frightened effort to stay the rush*] Eh !

[*As the Codger comes near to the window, Reiligan enters
on the path behind the wall, sees what is happening, and
stares across the wall in bewildered amazement.   The
Codger turns half-sides on reaching the window, hits it
with a bang, and the window bursts open, so that the
Codger, sack and all, goes on headlong into the room.*

Reiligan [*agonisingly*]. Oh, what's this, what's this ?
What's the rascal done ?   [*To the others*] You muted
jays, who ordered him to carry a sack of cement
through me grand drawin'-room ; over me carpet, me
new carpet, laid special for the Bishop ?   [*The Prodical
is busy with the wall, back turned to the world and Reiligan ;
Rankin, though working, is still praying ; Daniel is busy
stretching up from the ground to fumble with the bricks on
the scaffolding, his back, too, turned towards Reiligan.   All
remain silent.   Furious*] Answer !   One of yous !   Who
told the Codger to make a passage-way through me
drawing-room to carry stuff to the east side of the
house ?   [*Silence.   He pulls the Prodical off the scaffold.*]
Oh, come off the scaffold, an' answer me, man !

Prodical [*resentfully*]. He had to go somewhere !   He was
in before I started to wonder where he was goin' !

Daniel [*solemnly*]. He musta taken the wrong turnin'.

Reiligan [*still in agony*]. Ooh !   An' I wanted Keelin to
help in pluckin' fifty ducks for tomorrow's market !
Now, she'll be all night cleanin' me new carpet laid
down to make the world soft under the Bishop's feet !
[*He jumps up on to the platform, and pushes Rankin so
violently in the back that he is bent in two over the top of the
wall.*]   You, you prayin' gaum, you answer !

Rankin. I dunno ; I wasn't watchin'.

Reiligan [*shoving him aside — disgustedly*]. You prayer-gasper, if you prayed less, you'd see more ! [*He jumps from the scaffold, his glance catching sight of the bricks. He pulls Daniel over to them.*] Didn't I say them bricks were to be put behind the house ? Can't you see they're spoilin' the look of the lovely urn ? [*He looks into the urn.*] Oh, which of you monkey-souled jays are shovin' cigarette butts an' old papers into me garden urn, makin' a dust-bin of it ? [*He pushes Daniel's head down towards the urn.*] Looka there. Who threw them in ? D'ye hear me askin' ? Is your tongue palsied, or what ?

Daniel [*sullen*]. Eh, steady, there.

Reiligan [*furious*]. Clean it out, out, an' take the bricks away !
> [*Keelin appears at the window, her dress and her face dusty with dry cement. She has a sweeping-brush in her hand, and is half tearful.*

Keelin. What the hell did yous let the Codger do ? The carpet's half-way ruined, yella with cement ; dust over everything when the sack burst. The brush is no good — instead of brushin' it out, it brushes it in.
> [*She shakes the brush, and a cloud of cement dust floats into the garden.*

Reiligan. Clean it off, girl, clean it off ! Get the carpet clean, an' then go to give a hand to the pluckin' of the fifty ducks for tomorrow's market.

Keelin [*indignantly*]. I'll do no such thing. I've been long at you to get one of them machines pluckin' a bird in a few seconds that would take us an hour to do.

Reiligan [furious]. That's what yous all want — machines ! So's yous all can sit soft on your backsides watchin' the machines workin'. *[Angrily and impatiently]* Get the carpet done first, girl ; get the carpet clean !

Keelin. I don't know how I'm goin' to do it. It'll take me all night. It's in a terrible state. An' we're as bad. It's all in our eyes an' up our noses.

Reiligan [near out of his mind]. A terrible state ! *[To the others]* Didjas hear that, you bunch of destituted owls ! Near a ton of raw cement spilled over, lashed down, on me new carpet, an' not a soul of yous lifted a finger to save it ! Yous didn't hear, did yous ? *[In a great shout]* She'll be up all the night cleanin' it ! A new carpet that I had laid down so's the Bishop could walk over the room with dignity an' warmth. A carpet alight with colour an' alert with good taste.

Keelin [dolefully]. It'll never be the same carpet again.

Reiligan [in agony]. Never be the same carpet again ! Didjas hear that ? Not a sigh of a sound from any of yous ! An' I left the Codger quietly tossin' over the hay. *[He jumps on to the scaffold, catches Rankin by the shoulders, and shakes him.]* What was the Codger doin' here, what was the Codger doin' here ?

Rankin. I dunno ; he didn't say.

Reiligan. He didn't say, an' you didn't ask him. *[He grips the Prodical and shakes him.]* What was the Codger doin' here, you ?

Prodical [angrily]. How the hell do I know ?

Keelin [impatiently]. Aw, Da, for goodness' sake, send someone in to carry the Codger out, an' take away the burst bag before the cement eats into the carpet.

Reiligan [*furiously*]. Eatin' into it while yous stand there dodderin' into doin' nothin' to help. [*With a yell*] Go on, go on in, an' try to save what's left of me new carpet ! [*He pushes Prodical towards the window.*] Go on, you. [*He pushes Daniel towards the barrow.*] Get the barrow, man, to wheel the sack away. [*Daniel wheels the barrow to the window. The Prodical goes into the room. Rankin stays on the scaffold, his back turned towards the turmoil. Keelin lingers at the window. Reiligan in a rage jumps on to the scaffold, catches hold of Rankin, and pulls him on to the ground. Pushing Rankin towards the window*] Oh, you menacer, turn your face to where the trouble is, an' not be lardin' your skimpy soul with maudlin mumbles, settin' the saints above wonderin' why they aren't deaf. Come outa your booze of prayin' for a minute to help our christian humanity on its way !

[*Reiligan shoves him into the house after the Prodical. Daniel wheels the barrow to the window. Prodical and Rankin come out carrying the burst bag of cement which they place on the barrow, and Daniel wheels it away behind the house, past the ash tree, coming back to the garden with the barrow when he has left it there.*

[*As the work goes on, Foorawn comes past the ash tree, and comes out into the garden. As she comes out to the garden, Manus is following her but stops beside the ash tree, and leans against it, watching her. Prodical and Rankin have gone back into the house to get the Codger. Foorawn is tall and handsome, twenty-seven years of age. She has large blue eyes, brown hair that shows reddish gleams within it ; it is thick and long, and is pulled back from a white, narrow forehead, to be arranged in a thick bun resting on the nape of her white neck. She tries to give her fair face a look of resolute and austere serenity. She is dressed in a black, tailor-made suit, which is*

meant to be solemn and sober, but which plainly hints at
the slim, trim figure beneath it.   A thin gold chain en-
circles her neck, its two ends meeting to hold up a red
enamel cross hanging on her breast.   A blue mantle covers
part of her glossy brown hair, and a belt of the same
colour encircles her waist.   The men, whenever they pass
her, lift their hats respectfully in tribute to her reputa-
tion for piety, and in reverence for the vow of perpetual
chastity with which she has burdened herself.   She tries
to keep her eyes turned modestly towards the ground, but
doesn't always succeed, for her years are few and her heart
is young and yearning.   She looks the other way, but
steals a glance or two at Manus, then drops her look to the
ground at her feet again.

Foorawn [*to Reiligan*]. I'm goin', Da, to say a few short
   prayers to bless the Bishop's welcome. [*She notices his*
   agitation.]   What's goin' on here ?   What's happened ?

Reiligan [*to Foorawn — irritably*]. All right, all right, go,
   but get outa the way !   It's desolation's goin' on here,
   that's what ; so go on, you, for prayers are no use here
   now.

Manus [*loudly, and with some mockery in his voice, from his*
   place near the tree]. An' say a few, too, for the Bishop's
   bonfire !
      [*She flashes a timid and longing look at Manus, but quickly*
      lets her glance fall towards the ground again.

Foorawn [*to Reiligan*]. I won't be long, Da.
                              [*She goes out by the gate.*

Keelin [*as Foorawn goes towards the gate, and is walking off*
   behind the wall — maliciously]. If I know anything,
   there's silk knickers an' nylon stockin's under the

skirt that feels so sober an' looks so black. Why doesn't your old threadbare mouth order her to help a little about the house?

Reiligan [*angrily*]. You know why. She belongs to God, an' is separated from menial work — her for prayer an' you for work. [*More angrily*] Go in, I tell you, an' finish the carpet, an' then get on with the pluckin' of the ducks! [*He pushes her in.*]

    [*Now the Prodical and Rankin come out to the garden, helping the Codger out of the room. His face and clothes show how well the sack of cement had scattered its dust. They let him sink down to sit by the window, and recline himself against its sash. He reclines quiet, his eyes closed.*

Prodical [*advising*]. Leave him quiet, now, till he gets back his *status quo.*

Reiligan [*angrily — down to Codger*]. Why are you here? Why didn't you stay turnin' the hay? You knew what the turnip-fly has done — more than half the crop riddled an' useless. How'r we goin' to winter-feed the cattle without the good help of the hay? [*Shouting*] Why'd you come here to demonstrate destruction? Why didn't you stay with the hay?

Codger [*without the opening of an eye*]. God, he calls the hay hay!

Reiligan. Ay, an' prime hay too! Hay full of ripe juice got from the sun, purveyin' fat nourishment to me cattle, an' afterwards, fat nourishment to man through the milk the cattle give!

Codger [*wearily*]. Hay? Dust that the weary cattle can't chew. There isn't a sign in any meadow even of clover

or of vetch.   Meadows that haven't felt the rousin' rift
of a plough for fifty years.

Reiligan. It's my land, isn't it ?
  [*The Canon comes along behind the wall, and stops at the
  gate to listen.*

Codger [*eyes shut*]. Meadows a medley of mayweed an' of
  dock, with rushes creepin' in from the brook's bank.
  Grass that's tired of life before it's quarter grown.   He
  calls his cattle cattle !   The best of them cross-eyed
  with the strain of spillin' out a few hundred gallons a
  year ; spillin' out what all know is an illusion of what
  it ought to be ; with every passer-by turnin' his head
  aside so's not to see the tormented look on their gobs
  an' they complainin' silently to God against the dawn's
  lift-up of another day.

Reiligan. Even so, even if your lie was truth, it's me own
  loss, for I own them all.

Codger. You own them all.   You own the land, own the
  tavern, own the shirt factory, own the dance hall, own
  the store, an' God help us, you own the people too.
  You're a menace to the world, Reiligan.
  [*The Canon has come over from the gate, and now stands
  looking down on the shut-eyed Codger.*

Canon [*prodding Codger in the ribs with umbrella*]. What's
  that I hear you sayin', Codger Sleehawn, what's this I
  hear you sayin' ?   Why aren't you attendin' to the
  hay ?   To your master's hay ?

Codger [*with mock reverence*]. Oh ! the Canon's voice.   The
  Church an' State's gettin' together.   I was bearin' a
  bag of cement, Canon, an' some bum shoved me in the
  wrong direction.

Prodical [*who with Rankin has drifted back to working at the wall*]. He's a bit delirious.   After a little rest, Canon, he'll be back to his *status quo*.

Canon [*prodding the Codger again*]. Remember when you speak to Councillor in the future, you will be speaking to a Count, for His Holiness has honoured us all by making the Councillor a Count of the Papal Court.

Codger [*eyes still closed*]. A Count is it ?   [*Lifting his hat — with mock piety*] Ballyoonagh lifts herself up a step nearer to heaven !

Canon [*roughly*]. An' no more talk, Sleehawn, about the Count's land or the Count's cattle; or his good hay either.

Codger [*a touch of mockery in his tone of voice*]. Good land, Canon, an' finest hay I've seen in a generation ; nothin' like it, caught in the urge of the sun an' yieldin' to the tender kiss of the dews the nights give. [*He sniffs.*]   I can get the smell of the hay from here : fuller an' sweeter than any scent from a far-off land where there's camphor an' rare gums tricklin' from the trees, givin' a forest all the grandeur of a grove of roses bushed about with thyme.
  [*Father Boheroe comes to the window with a glass of liquor in his hand.   He offers it to the Codger.*

Father Boheroe [*offering glass to Codger*]. Keelin sent this out to you.

Codger [*shrinking*]. What is it — water ?

Father Boheroe. No, no : the best of brandy.

Reiligan [*dismayed*]. Brandy ? Is it the Bishop's brandy — Good God !   That damned girl !   To give the like of that brandy to the like of him !
  [*He rushes into the house.*

Codger [*taking the glass eagerly*]. A grand girl, God bless her ! The scent of camphor and thyme is in her goodness, an' her look in the morning, or when the evenin' comes, is as the simple grandeur of Sharon's rose ; ay, an' her comin' an' goin' carries grace along, and is lure enough to make a man turn his head to look, an' his mind to a grabbin' thought to get her.

Canon [*quietly — to Father Boheroe*]. He didn't need brandy. I wish, when you get a chance, Father [*indicating the Codger*], you'd put a curb on this mischievous old mouth.

Father Boheroe. It may be a disturbing old mouth, Canon ; but I wouldn't say it was a mischievous one.

Canon [*impatiently, but quietly*]. Your parish Priest says it is mischievous, and it is — mischievous and unruly.

Father Boheroe. We have authority, Canon, for believing that old men may sometimes see visions ; and what the Codger sees has been seen by others.

Canon [*about to enter house*]. Visions ? The Codger's visions are compounded of ignorant and impudent guff. Visions, me neck ! [*A pause.*] And look, Father Boheroe, a priest would do well to beware of seeking promotion in his mind from spiritual ambition ; and hesitate before he hangs a tassel of honour upon any emotional fancy. Please come in, Father Boheroe. Looks as if I had more than one mischievous and unruly man in my parish.

[*They both go in.*

Codger [*scornfully*]. A Count ! His Holiness honours Ballyoonagh be makin' Reiligan a Count. A Count, be God ! [*He holds his glass of liquor out from him, and calls*]

Dan ! [*Daniel turns towards him, as Rankin suddenly gets off the scaffold, and goes out by the gate, his hat off, his head bent in prayer. Fervently*] Happiness to Miss Keelin Reiligan and [*he pauses*] to another ! [*He drinks.*] Prime stuff. Bishop's brandy, right enough. [*He utters a half-cry*] Jasus, me back aches ! [*A pause.*] Count Mick — can you imagine it !

Prodical [*in a listening attitude*]. Whisht ! The Angelus ! You can hear it faintly when the breeze blows this way.
> [*Indeed, the sound of the bell is faintly heard at irregular intervals till the twelve strokes are struck.*

Daniel [*indignantly*]. An' the louser, Rankin, heard it, and left, without sayin' a word.

Manus [*who has been standing by the tree, drinking from a mug*]. Blow for lunch, lads. And there's more in the keg, if any of you'd like a cooler ; with a bottle of the Bishop's brandy in it to give the drink a body : for they shall not muzzle the oxen that are treadin' out the corn.
> [*He comes over to the heap of bricks, and sits down on them.*
> [*The rest eagerly make for the way to the keg, marching not quite so stiffly as before ; but still with signs of exaltation, the Codger bringing up the rear. He pauses at the tree, and turns towards Manus.*

Codger [*to Manus*]. Aren't you comin' too ?

Manus [*quietly*]. I'll join you in a few minutes, old friend.

Codger [*softly and feelingly*]. Waitin' for a chance to see her. A union would be a blossomy blessin' to yous both. May God smile on you, Manus, and the lassie too. Waitin' is hard an' watchin' is hard and wonderin' is harder still. [*A pause.*] A Count, be God !
> [*He goes.*

[*Foorawn comes in by the path behind the wall, comes through the gateway, sees Manus, goes a little aside to avoid him, but he moves, too, and the two of them stand face to face; he looking steadily at her, she, after a long glance, turning her gaze to the ground, pulling her mantle more closely round her face.*]

Manus. Foorawn !

Foorawn [*in a slightly frightened voice*]. Oh, Manus, don't stop me ; let me go quietly in for both our sakes. I never thought I'd meet you.

Manus [*firmly*]. You knew I'd be near. You saw me as you were going. You hoped to meet me. You wanted to meet me. You meant to meet me !

Foorawn. No, no, I didn't. When you stopped me yesterday, I beseeched you not to trouble me again.

Manus. You wanted to see me yesterday ; you wanted to see me today. You would like to see me till your eyes were old, and could see no more.

Foorawn [*poignantly*]. God forgive me ! Don't torment me, Manus. Let me go quietly into my refuge. I am now under the pure white moon of heaven. Gone for ever from you, Manus. Look at me all in black an' blue. I am no longer a lure to your seeking eyes.

Manus. Oh, you cannot hide the lure of your figure under a tenebrae cloak, or masquerade your handsome face under a hiding hood. Oh, Foorawn, my love and my longing for you go under them all.

Foorawn. Go away from me ! I prayed to help you on your way to the priesthood ; and while I was praying, you were creeping from your intention during the slow, cold hours of an early morning, leaving your name marked down as dead in the sacred register of the College ; an' then, an' then you ran off to become one of the English air force.

Manus. Where I flew towards death at every chance I got so that I might die from all that had happened ; but God laughed, and presented me with a medal ; and when in another chance, I pushed closer to death, He laughed again, and added a silver bar to ripen the ribbon.

Foorawn. Look at you now ; oh, look at you now !

Manus. Yes, look at me now. [*He takes her arm gently, and draws her towards him.*] A man with the same soul, the same mind, the same defiance of shabby life [*he gathers her into his arms*], and the same outlasting and consuming love for Foorawn, my [*he kisses her*] own, and for ever.

Foorawn [*pulling herself out of his arms*]. No, no ! I must go. I belong to God now, and Him only can I serve.

Manus [*bitterly*]. That's pride and fear speaking. You think God couldn't do without you ; at a loss when He can't find you. Go on, then, heaping up pound after pound for foreign missions that bring a sly storm of harm to the ebonised African in the sun's centre, and the icy-homed Eskimo in the shroudy snows of the north.

Foorawn [*halting at the window — surprised*]. What pounds are you talking about ?

Manus. The notes heaped up for the good greed of the church in the bureau-drawer under the votive light. The key's under your bodice on your breast within where the cross is lying on your breast without. [*Bitterly*] Cross and key to keep you cold, lying where my hand ought to be to keep you warm.

Foorawn [*coldly*]. Your words are wild and your words are bitter. Your words are like the words in the books that will burn to ashes in the Bishop's bonfire. Manus, you are a bad man.

Manus [*bitterly*]. And in the ashes that the fire will leave will be the ashes of our love ; of mine for you, of yours for me ; and Daniel's love for Keelin and hers for him.

Foorawn [*going in by the window*]. A very bad man !
    [*Manus makes to go after her angrily, but finds Father Boheroe standing in his way. They face each other for a moment, then Manus turns and goes slowly back to the heap of bricks to sit down on them, resting his head in his hands.*

Father Boheroe [*from near the window — softly*]. Be a man, Manus. She is too deep now in the vainglory of her chastity to come to you.

Manus [*impatiently*]. Oh, you ! You who stifle and tangle people within a laocoön of rosary beads !

Father Boheroe. I wish, not to tangle them with rosary beads, Manus, but to join them with life. . . . Come, let yourself fall in love with life, and be another man.

Manus [*sarcastically*]. At peace with all things.

Father Boheroe. At war with most things.

Manus. You are a kind, good man, Father. [*He pauses.*] Would you do me a great favour ?

Father Boheroe [*eagerly*]. Of course I would. You've but to tell me what it is, Manus.

Manus [*tonelessly*]. Just leave me alone.

> [*Father Boheroe goes slowly to the gate, opens it, and passes out to the path behind the wall. He halts there, leaning thoughtfully over the wall's top.*
>
> [*The others, Prodical, Daniel, and Codger, come back to the garden by the ash tree, the Codger leading, the butt of the hay-fork's handle in his hand, the prongs trailing along the ground behind him. His eyes are glazed and dreamy, but he walks more erect than ever, though his steps, now and again, are unsteady. He goes to the heap of bricks and sits down on them, on the opposite side from Manus, so that his head or hat is only seen, with the hay-fork, prongs upward, rising up beside him like a trident. Daniel goes over to the gate, walking more stiffly than before, and stands there looking pensively out over the fields. The Prodical goes over to the scaffold, and sits down upon it, head erect and eyes alight with an inarticulate defiance of the world.*

Prodical [*to the world and to Father Boheroe*]. Prodical Carranaun demands a wider world, Father Boheroe ; a world where a man can roar his real opinions out ; where night becomes a generous part of a day, where rough seas tumble in on a lonely shore. Prodical Carranaun is far above the meanin' of Reiligan's roses and Reiligan's wall !

Daniel [*gazing out over the fields — half to himself*]. I'm in a mood for work no longer. Let work go hang. I'll go stretch meself in a meadow, an' go listen, listen to the lark singin'. The lark, wha' ? Yes, the lark singin' in the clear air, clear air of the day, wha' ?

Codger [*musingly*]. You do well, Dan. The lark's a bonnie
bird ; our Lady's hen singin' near all the year round.
But for all her singin', the lark has her troubles like
the rest of us, a lot of sorra ; all kinds, like the rest of
us. Even in love when she waits an' waits an' waits
for the mate that sometimes never comes back to the
nest. An' we're all like the birds that way : sorra
after the loved one's gone outa sight or gone from ken.
Father Boheroe there could tell you that. [*After a pause,
he lilts quietly and softly :*]

My Bonnie's gone over the ocean, my Bonnie's gone
    over the sea ;
My Bonnie's gone over the ocean, Oh, bring back my
    Bonnie to me.

  [*Daniel and the Prodical join the Codger in the chorus —
  Daniel at the chorus's second line, the Prodical at the
  third, so that from the third line they are singing
  together ; Father Boheroe listening as he leans by the
  gate ; Manus sitting lonely on the bricks ; his hands
  under the chin of his bent head.*]

Bring back, bring back,

                               [*Daniel joining in.*
Oh, bring back my Bonnie to me, to me ;

                               [*Prodical joining in.*
Bring back, bring back,
Oh, bring back my Bonnie to me.

END OF ACT I

ACT II

The drawing-room of Councillor Reiligan's house is a large one, and everything in it is new, except the things that are newer, and the newest that are now being added to adorn the Bishop's stay. At the back is the big bow-window, black plushy curtains at either side, with a white pelmet over them, looking out to the garden, and we can see from it a wide and elegant branch of the ash tree, beginning to look black in the deepening dusk; the heap of bricks is there too, and the urn in front of them. Behind them all is the wall and the gateway, the path behind it, and the fields stretching away to the town. The window through which people come and go is open to the garden, for the evening is fine and balmy though the autumn is wending a way to its ending. Some few birds are still faintly twittering, and at some distance the cawing cries of the rooks are heard, not loud, but clear, flying home for rest and sleep. All is calm and peaceful without, though there is bustle and some anxious hurryings within.

To the right of the window is an upright piano, covered with an old sheet, and another sheet covers a big sideboard to the left of the window. On a ledge, or bracket, beside the piano, is a telephone. A table to seat six or seven stands somewhat to the middle of the room; it is a mahogany one, and has been polished so that the surface shines like a brightened mirror. There are six or so chairs set round the room, their seats cushioned with dark-green cloth, mahogany-backed and mahogany-legged.

The fireplace, a large and wide one, is to the right, and is curbed by a shining brass fender with heavy, brightened brass poker, tongs, and coal-shovel. There are paper and sticks and coal set there so that a great blazing fire may be kindled any minute in the grate to warm up a room that is used only to

46

*receive important visitors.   The mantelpiece has a two-set piece
of prancing bronze horses, one at either end, and in the centre a
gilded clock that does go.   Over them, on the wall, is a big
picture of a Pope which Reiligan says is a striking likeness of Pio
Nino.   Between the piano and the window is a narrow bureau,
also of mahogany, with narrow drawers, and a desk-like top.   It is
half a prie-dieu, for a ledge for kneeling juts out at the bottom,
softened for kneeling by a black-covered cushion.   Over this, on
the wall, is a bracket holding a votive-light ; above, on a smaller
bracket, is the small statue of Saint Casabianca, who has a black
face, wears a scarlet robe, and carries a golden crown in one hand.
Over the floor is a thick beige carpet, partly covered with old
sheets, particularly giving a protective covering to the carpet from
the door to the right of the fireplace, leading to the rest of the
house, and the door on left, leading to the kitchen basement, the
hall, and the front entrance.*

At one end of the table are writing-paper, pen, and ink.

*When we see the scene, we find Rankin looking down at the
hearthstone, once a plain slab of slate, now a gorgeous hearthstone
of green, yellow, and white tiles that he has laid there.   He has
a trowel in one hand, a chamois-cloth in the other.   The Codger
is carrying out a mortar-board by the window.   Rankin bends
down, and gives the tiles another polish with the cloth.*

Rankin [*to the Codger*]. You can tell them they can light
   the fire now any time they like.   It's all firmly set.

Codger. It needs one.   With all its newness, the room's
   musty, and with all its image and its holy picture, it
   smells of mercy as much as the County Court.
   [*The Codger goes out by the window with the mortar-board ;
   Rankin goes to the window and peeps out after him,
   then slides to the bureau, and, taking away the kneeling-
   cushion that lies before it, kneels down on the ledge to
   pray.*

Rankin [*scornfully as he removes the cushion*]. Cushion !
[*Softly and with suppressed intensity*] Holy Saint Casabianca
of Allahoona, pray for us, that Ballyoonagh may be
blessed by the Bishop's comin' soona —
> [*The door to the right flies open, and in rushes Lieutenant
> Michael Reiligan.   He is in full marching order, steel
> helmet, English pattern, dark-green uniform, Sam Browne
> belt, sword slung on one side, revolver in holster on the
> other.*

Lieutenant [*breathlessly*]. Where's me Da ; did you see me
oul' fella ?

Rankin [*who has jumped up to his feet — sheepishly*]. I dunno ;
no, I dunno. [*The Lieutenant flies out by the door on left.
Rankin tiptoes to it, peeps out after the officer, closes it carefully,
returns to the prie-dieu, kneels down again, and begins to pray.
Praying*] Holy Saint Casabianca of Allahoona, pray for
us that the Bishop's bonfire may light such a flame in
Ballyoonagh soona —
> [*The door on the left flies open, and Keelin rushes into the
> room. Rankin springs to his feet, and stands sheepishly
> near to the prie-dieu.*

Keelin [*breathlessly*]. Didja see me Da? Where's the
Count Reiligan ?

Rankin. I dunno, Miss Keelin ; no, I dunno.

Keelin [*petulantly*]. Looks like this Bishop's visit is goin'
to be a curse instead of a blessin' !
> [*She rushes out by the door on the right, leaving it open
> after her.   Rankin tiptoes over to it, peeps out, returns to
> the prie-dieu, kneels down, and begins to pray again.*

Rankin [*praying*]. Holy Saint Casabianca of Allahoona,
pray for us that the Bishop's bonfire may light such a

blaze in all the hearts in Ballyoonagh that men may no longer think of women, or women think of men, soona —

[*Count Reiligan, still in his morning suit and top hat, appears at the window, stares at Rankin for a moment, and then flares into indignation.*

Reiligan [*angrily*]. What the hell are you doing at that pray doo ? [*As Rankin jumps up, frightened and embarrassed*] That pray doo is the private perquisite of Miss Foorawn, and not meant for one of your stattus. [*He comes closer to Rankin.*] That's Miss Foorawn's special Saint ; [*indicating statue*] an' no one in the house prays to him but her. See ? Understand ? [*As Rankin remains silent, with bent head*] Oh, for God's sake, man, say something, so's I'll know you savee !

Rankin [*feebly*]. Yis.

Reiligan. Yis what ?

Rankin [*with rising falsetto*]. I understand !

Reiligan [*roughly*]. Well, then, try to act accordin' ! Even Miss Foorawn herself has decided not to use it while the Bishop's living here for two or three nights as his headquarters. Get that ? [*He waves a hand round the room*] This whole room's the Bishop's perquisite while he's here, and we're relegatin' the room and all that's in it to the Bishop's stattus, furnishin' him with a sittin'-room an' private oratorium for his security and comfort while his stay honours our much-loved town of Ballyoonagh. Understand ? [*Impatiently — as Rankin stays silent*] Oh, for God's sake, say something to show you savee !

Rankin [*very lowly*]. Yis.

Reiligan [*shouting*]. Yis what, man ! Yis which !

Rankin [*shouting in falsetto*]. Yis that ! I understand !

Religan [*shouting*]. Well, act accordin' then. [*Looking at the hearth*] Ah, now that's lookin' fine now ! You're done here, so come along an' help with the paintin' of the hall. You're done here, so come on. [*Pushing him*] Oh, on, on ; no dilly-dallying !
[*As they are about to go out by the door on the left, Daniel appears at the opposite door. He is carrying a square pedestal of polished black wood with a raised circular rim within its top, evidently there to make a statue's stand secure.*]

Daniel. Here, Count, is the box for the Saint somebody or other to stand on.

Reiligan. Put it on the table. [*As Daniel dumps it near the edge — angrily*] Gently, you careless tit, an' don't scratch me table. In the centre, you fool ; in the centre of the table !

Rankin [*imitating in falsetto*]. In the centre of the table, fool !

Reiligan [*impatiently pushing Rankin out by the door, and following him*]. Oh, you ! Interferin' gob, you ! What's it to you whether it's in the centre or at the side ? Oh, come you an' help with the painting of the hall ! I've told you before ; I'm tellin' you again, we've no use now for a dilly-dallier !
[*As Daniel measures the pedestal into the perfect centre of the table, Lieutenant Reiligan comes in by the door on right, and for a moment watches Daniel's manœuvres.*]

Lieutenant [*cordially*]. Hello, Dan, me son.

Daniel [*turning round — more cordially*]. Oh, hello, Mick.
  [*The Lieutenant crosses the room and hangs the holstered
  revolver by its sling from a hook in the wall to the left of
  the votive-light.*

Lieutenant. This thing's rubbin' me hip. It'll be safe here,
Dan. Should be beside a saint.

Daniel. Dunno, Mick, if it's always safe to leave a gun
within reach of a saint these days.

Lieutenant [*laughingly*]. Now, Dan, no mockery ! Seen
me oul' feller anywhere ?

Daniel [*as cautiously*]. Just gone out be that door.

Lieutenant. What sort of a gob had he on him ? Gay, or
what ?

Daniel. Uneasy. He's feelin' the flow of the money away
from him. All he's spendin' on the Bishop's the core
in the talk of the town. All he's doin' and all he's
bringin' to diversify the house is the centre, too, of the
town's sight an' hearin', like a rocket of coloured stars
let loose in a deep dark sky.

Lieutenant [*as confidently as he can*]. He'll spend a little
more when I get to him, for I must find a tenner somewhere.

Daniel. A tenner ? Why only a tenner ? Why not tap
him for more than a tenner ? A tenner won't go far.

Lieutenant. Ay, Dan, for with me an officer in charge of
the Guard of Honour to meet the Bishop, an' the glory
hangin' round the house now, I have to keep up my
stattus in the Officers' Mess.

Daniel [*emphatically*]. Of course you have ! You need to
keep a Guard of Honour round your stattus.

Lieutenant [*as emphatically*]. An' I'm goin' to ! A waterfall of money flowin' for a Bishop, an' him denyin' his son a tiny tenner ; his own son, mind you, Dan.

Daniel. His own son : yis, I know, I know. It's little short of a visible mystery, Mick.
  [*The Codger comes in by the door on right carrying a pot of green paint in one hand and a big paint-brush in the other. He appears almost at the same moment as the Prodical is seen at the window, carrying a huge duck, fully plucked, and ready for roasting, on a wide dish. The Codger halts at one end of the table, Prodical at the other.*

Prodical. The finest duck of the fifty for the Bishop.

Lieutenant [*somewhat enviously*]. Looks like they're goin' to regale the laddo with a whole regalia of things. Must be costin' the oul' fella a packet. An' his own son shakin' a shillin' in a pocket.

Codger. Bill Mullarkey under a bishop's robe's a different one to the one I knew with a patch on the seat of his trousers. Makes a helluva difference when the hand that held a hay-fork now grips a crozier ! An' withal his golden mitre and his purple petticoat, he's Bill Mullarkey still.

Lieutenant [*to Daniel who is polishing the pedestal with a cloth*]. What's that there you're polishin' ?

Daniel. A stand for a big statue, coloured fair an' gilded nobly, of some saint that no mortal in Ireland never heard of.

Codger. The one thing increasin' in Ireland — the population of stone an' wooden saints.

Lieutenant. What's his name ? Maybe I'd know the fella.

Daniel. I was told it, but it's gone outa me mind now. A curious name — something concerned with a bugle or something.

Lieutenant. A bugle ? How could it be a bugle ?

Daniel [*thinking*]. Some kinda musical thing it was anyway.

Codger [*prompting*]. Fiddle, drum, cornet ?

Lieutenant. Saxophone, oboe ?

Prodical [*placing his duck on the table as the Codger has already placed his pot of paint and his brush*]. Dulcimer, maybe ?

Daniel [*thinking hard*]. Wait now — let me think ; yes, the fella was a soldier who played a buck, a buckineeno in the old Roman Army.

Codger. An' what kinda spiritual stir is a sinner's goin' to get out of a buckineeno. Somethin' sinister in it to me. We'll be all well served with a Bishop an' a buckineeno.

Daniel [*in an air of great secrecy*]. Hush ! Listen ! No word to go from here. The buckineeno boyo is the private patron of the Bishop, and his statue always fronts him while he's thinkin'. If he's thinkin' right, the buckineeno blows a steady note ; if his thinkin's goin' wrong, the buckineeno quavers. The Canon told the Count, Count told Foorawn, Foorawn told Keelin, an' Keelin told me.

Prodical [*snorting contemptuously*]. Pah !

Daniel. What are you pahhin' outa you for, Prodical ! Looka the way this house has prospered be the prayers made to Saint Casabianca be Miss Foorawn.
[*He gestures towards the statue on the bracket over the bureau.*

Prodical [*taking up the dish and the duck, and about to go out*].
Pah !

Codger. Buckineeno or no buckineeno, clear or quaverin',
I can't see Bill Mullarkey thinkin' at all.

Daniel [*resentfully*]. There's more in it than Pah ! The
way the country's in, we need all the help we can get
from the saints.

Lieutenant. That's all right — up to a point, Dan ; but
what we want now is soldiers an' not saints. How best
are we goin' to act if tens of thousands of Russian paratroopers came droppin' down from the Irish skies on
to Tara's Hill or the Mountains of Mourne. You
haven't to think twice to see the pickle we'd be in then.

Codger. It would be better an' fitter for us to guard against
the swarms of green flies an' swarms of black flies that
drop from our Irish skies, an' slaughter the crops.

Daniel [*indignantly — to Codger*]. Aw, don't be an eejut.
Go on, Mick.

Lieutenant. You see, Dan, we're too small to fight the
Russians on our own — we'd have to have help.

Daniel. We're twice too small — we'd have to have help :
you're right there.

Lieutenant. No use, either, of looking to allies too far off,
like Italy or France — they'd take years to come.

Prodical [*who has become interested, and has placed the duck
and the dish back on the table again*]. So they would, so
they would.

Lieutenant. You see, men, Ireland's so important, geo-
graphically, that, in a war, the Russians would need to

take her over within an hour, within an hour.   Does
that ring a bell ?

Daniel [*convinced*]. Yis ;   a whole peal of them.   But
then, wha' ?

Lieutenant. Well, man, we'd have to get help at once.

Prodical. Then what about England ?

Lieutenant. England ! Why, man alive, she'd be fightin' for
her life, an' couldn't let us have even a policeman from
point-duty !   I'm an Army Officer ;   I know these things.

Daniel [*wisely — to Prodical*]. You see, Prodical ?   He's
an Army Officer — he knows.   [*To Lieutenant*] Well,
then, wha', Mick ?

Lieutenant. America's our only man, Dan, for what we
need is swarms an' swarms of jeeps.

Codger [*incredulous*]. Jeeps ?

Lieutenant. Yes, jeeps ;   each with a driver, a spare driver,
a commander, an' a wireless operator.   Every able-
bodied man in Ireland in a jeep here an' a jeep there,
with a sten-gun, a hammer an' pliers, head-phone, an'
a jeepsie walkie-talkie — that's the one solution, Dan.

Codger [*testily*]. An' what would the ordinary cars an'
pedestrians do, an' the roads buzzin' with jeeps ?
There wouldn't be a man, woman, child, or chicken
left alive in the country !

Daniel [*rapping the table*]. Order, order, Codger ;   order !

Lieutenant [*hotly — to the Codger*]. An' even if they were all
done in aself, wouldn't death on our own roads be
better than exportation be the Bolsheviks to an unknown
destination ?

Codger. What exportation are you walkie-talkiein' about ?

Daniel. Don't talk like an eejut, Codger.

Lieutenant [*hotly*]. Looka, a nation like Russia that did so much to her own people wouldn't cast a thought about eliminatin' a few thousand Irishmen an' Irish-women, or wait to think twice about exportin' the rest of us.

Codger [*fiercely*]. An' where would the Bolsheviks find the ships an' trains to export four millions of us ? Siberia's a long way off, if you ask me !

Lieutenant [*to the Codger*]. Looka, man, the Bolsheviks wouldn't be dreamin' of Siberia, an' the Isle of Man only a few feet away from our own green border.

Daniel [*to Codger*]. Aha, that's bet you ! You see, now, Codger, don't you ?

Codger [*vehemently*]. No, I don't see now ! If Russia be anything like what the clergy make it out to be, any Russians flutterin' down from the Irish skies on to our emerald sod will be poor divils seekin' an asylum.

Prodical. An asylum ? It's a lunatic asylum you must be meanin' ?

Codger [*rattily*]. No, no, man ; an ordinary asylum, an ordinary asylum !

Prodical. There's no ordinary asylum. When anyone says We've taken a certain party to the asylum, we mean a lunatic asylum, don't we ?

Codger. Yes, yes ; but——

Prodical. There's no but about it. An asylum's an asylum — there's no but about it.

Codger [*raising his voice*]. I'm tellin' you, there's different asylums ; for instance, a deaf an' dumb asylum !

Prodical [*raising his voice higher than the Codger*]. The paratroopers droppin' from our skies won't be deaf an' dumb, will they ?

Daniel [*louder than the other two*]. Order, order — let Mick speak !

Lieutenant [*resignedly*]. Aw, let the eejuts talk, Dan.

Prodical [*angrily — to the Lieutenant*]. Eejut yourself ! Wantin' to flood the country with jeeps ! Will you tell us who's goin' to provide the hundreds of thousands of jeeps to go gallopin' round, an' lay out every man-jack an' every woman-lizzie of us, dead as mackerel on the roads of Eireann, bar the boyos who have the good fortune to be sittin' in them ?

Codger [*fiercely — to Lieutenant*]. An' if we put into every one of them a driver, a spare driver, a commander, and a wireless operator with his walkie-talkie, addin' all them laid out flat an' dead on the roads, will you tell us who's goin' to look after the common things that have to be done to keep the country goin' ?

Prodical [*to Lieutenant*]. Aha, you're silent now. That's bet you !

Lieutenant [*in a rage as he goes swift from the room, banging the door after him*]. Aw, go to hell, you pair of eejuts !

Codger. You see, he turns to abuse when he's bet. Couldn't face up to unconfutable arguments.

Prodical. Him an' his jeeps ! Another thing — while America might be droppin' the jeeps, what's to prevent

the Bolshies at the same time from droppin' their para-
troops an' fillin' the jeeps as they touch down, to let
them go scamperin' all over the roads ?

Codger [*emphatically*]. Nothin'.   An', maybe, takin' over
the Turf Board, the Tourist Association, the Hospitals
Sweep, the Catholic Young Men's Society, the Protestant pulpits, an' the President's residence ; endin',
maybe, with the plantin' of a Red Flag in the hand of
Saint Patrick's Statue standin' helpless on a windy hill
in the centre of the lonely Plains of Meath !

Daniel. Don't be actin' the eejut, Codger !

Codger [*angrily*]. Who's actin' the eejut ?

Daniel [*as angrily*]. You are, the way you're talkin' !

Codger [*close up to him*]. Eejut yourself !

Daniel [*placing a hand to Codger's chest, and shoving him backwards*]. Aw, go away !

Codger [*rushing back, putting a hand to Daniel's chest, and
shoving him backwards*]. You go away !

Daniel [*swiftly returning, and giving the Codger a fiercer shove
backwards*]. You go away !

Prodical [*remonstrating*]. Gentlemen, easy !   Can't yous see
yous are turnin' your own opinions into *ipso factos* ?
    [*The door to the right suddenly opens, and Reiligan, with
    Foorawn behind him, comes into the room.   When he sees
    the three men, a look of surprised anger floods over his face.*

Reiligan [*angrily*]. What's this, aw, what's all this ?   The
bricks, too, left lyin' still in me garden !   Good
God, is this the way you're helpin' the work to welcome
the Bishop ?   Looka the paint on the mahogany table,

and the Bishop's duck beside it suckin' in the fumes,
with the hall little more than half painted, an' all hands
wanted to give the finishin' touches to the Bishop's
bonfire. You know we haven't a single minute to spare,
not a single minute, mind yous. From this out, there's
to be no talkin' ; and if anyone does talk, everybody
is to listen to nobody. Anyone — no one — mind
yous ! [*The three men stand mute.*] Damn it, are yous
listenin' to me ?

Codger. Damn it, you ; weren't you after sayin' no one
was to listen to no one.

Reiligan [*wildly*]. Not to me ; I'm not no one ! Not to
me. Yous are all to listen to me. Nobody's to listen
to anyone, but everybody's to listen to me !

Codger [*mockingly serious*]. Listen to him, lads ; yous are
all to listen to him.

Reiligan [*with a roar — to Prodical*]. Take the duck down
to the cook ! [*A roar — to Daniel*] Take the paint to
Rankin in the hall !
  [*A Railway Porter appears at the window ; a middle-aged
  man with whiskers under his chin, a wide mouth, and
  spectacles helping a pair of weak eyes. He is dressed in
  yellow or black corduroy trousers, the same material in
  a cotton-sleeved waistcoat, and he wears a peaked cap,
  circled by a red band, on his head. He looks worn out,
  and there is a settled look of fright on his face. He leans
  against the window's side, half-way into the room, half-
  way out of it. His eyes twitch open, twitch shut again,
  many times, rapidly, and he is out of breath for a time.
  Prodical, on his way out with the duck, and Daniel with
  the paint, pause, and stay to listen, one putting the paint
  back on the table, and the other putting back the duck.*]

Reiligan [*impatiently*]. What is it ?   What is it you want ?
What d' yeh want ?

Porter [*panting*]. Give a man a breeze, man !

Reiligan [*after a pause, while they look at him for a few moments*].
Well, me man, what do you want ?   Have you a message
or wha' ?

Porter [*half to himself*]. All right in a praying procession,
but weighin' heavy on the poor shoulder of your own
responsibility.   Poor sinner, poor sinner that I am !
Him irksome to me, me irksome to him.   He knew I
was a toss-up for heaven or hell ; head or a harp.   So
he kept blowin' ; oh, me poor ears — a piercin' blast !
[*A fierce blast from a horn or a cornet is heard by the Porter.*]
Just like that !

Reiligan [*mystified*]. Just like what ?

Porter [*ignoring him*]. Ran all the way to the polis station
to get shut of him.   Had his hooks dug into me from
start to finish.   [*Pressing his hands over his ears*] Oh, me
ears !   Buzzin' brazen still.   Every time I thought of
a drink, or a comic line from a song, he plunged the
bell over me ear, an' blew his best.

Reiligan. Blew his best ?   Who did ?

Foorawn. Who blew his best ?

Porter [*wistfully*]. He did.

Reiligan. Who did ?

Porter. He did.   Loud an' long, or sudden, sharp, an'
sinister.

Codger [*impatiently*]. Who blew long an' loud ?   Shake
yourself, Hughie Higgins, shake yourself, man !

Reiligan. Who blew sharp, sudden, an' sinister?

Porter. He did : the one with the big, big body an' the little, little head ; knocked me outa me downy dream ; the boyo with the bookaneeno.

Reiligan. Boyo with the bookaneeno?

Foorawn. The bookaneeno?

Prodical. Bookaneeno?

Porter. Them they call saints is right enough on a pedestal, half-hidden in a church frustrated with its own dimness ; but out in the light, they're dazzlin', an' there's danger in the dimension of their shinin'. Dimpled dangers the lot of them. [*With conviction*] No, no ; I'd rather look for heaven in a cracked lookin'-glass at home. I'm breathin' quiet now at last. We're both safe now : me here, him in the polis station waitin' for someone to carry him home here. [*In an awed whisper*] Whistist, the lot of yous carefully ; a question : is this bookaneeno boyo goin' to be a fixture in Ballyoonagh? I'd like to be warned.

Reiligan [*still mystified*]. Looka, me man, what are you complainin' of, an' what's the matter with you?

Porter [*to Reiligan*]. An' with you, too? What's the matter with you an' me is a world's question. We're all flyin' about on consequential an' bewildered wings. Even when singin' a song, a man's a sighin' sinner. A little whiskey now would buoy me up, and make me fancy meself safe in the world's welter.

Foorawn [*severely*]. There's no whiskey in this house for you, an' better for you if there was none outside of it either.

Porter [*quietly resentful*]. Whatever whiskey I take is got in your own Da's tavern, Miss. No whiskey in the house ; no nothin' ; no light in a window, no welcome at a door. [*To Foorawn*] I don't want to listen to you ; don't want to go too near to you, for you're one of the higher ones hearin' woe in the first cry comin' from a cradle. They're queer, these holy men an' holy women. Never have a minute's peace if you let them get you thinkin'. Give one of them ones a chance to get a grip on you, an' he'll have you worryin' God for help to do what you should be damn well able to do yourself without botherin' God at all.

Foorawn [*thrusting herself forward*]. You're speakin' blasphemy !

Prodical [*echoing her*]. Yis — blasphemy.

Codger. If you ask me, the poor man's beginnin' to say sense at last !

Daniel [*firmly*]. Hush, Codger ! We've got to be careful. A holy house has unholy enemies.

Reiligan [*finding an excuse*]. It's drink. He's not himself. He's coloured his mind with drink, and it's separatin' into pictures like ones in a stained-glass winda. It's drink.

Porter. An' what else have we ; we who see nothin', we who hear nothin' ; an' work hard : what else have we but drink to give us a coloured dream or two ?

Foorawn. You have prayer, bad man.

Porter [*suddenly coming to alert life, and standing full front before the crowd, waving his hands excitedly, moving a step forward, a step back, a step forward again*]. Listen, you blatherers ! A question for yous, a question ! Does a prayer lift you up or get you down ? Are these prayin' people right an' proper in a world like this at all ? How'd you like one of them to start on you, an' you sittin', glass in hand, listenin' to some gazebo singin' a shut-eyed song ? Or one of them with a hand on your shoulder, freezin' a body, an' you trying to shout victory to your county football team ? Would you feel at ayse to shout ? I'm a wild man when I think of these things. I'm askin' yous something, Is prayer good for you ? I don't mean the odd nod of the head most of us give to God, but the prayer that's the real McCoy — does it lift a man up, or does it cast a man down ? [*They stand, as they have stood for some time, in a semicircle around him, gaping, stiff and still, only moving back a step or two when he has come closer, waving his hands.*] There's no answer ; [*in a wail*] there's no answer ! We don't feel comfortable with them here, we won't feel comfortable with them there. What are we doin' but weavin' a way through life, content with an odd prayer to propel us towards where none of us wants to go ! How'r we to know if we're comin' up upstream, or goin' down downstream ? [*He catches sight of the big duck on the dish on the table.*] Jasus ! Who owns the massive duck ?

Reiligan [*breaking from the spell — angrily, to Prodical*]. Didn't I tell you long ago to take the Bishop's duck to the cook, an' not leave it exposed to the gaze of the whole world ? Take it down ! [*To Daniel*] An' you take that pot of paint to where the hall's bein' done, an' then put your uniform an' slippers on so's you'll be used to them when the time comes to act. [*To the*

Porter] An' you, get out and bring here whatever you left at the Polis Station.

[*Prodical goes out with the duck ; Daniel goes out with the paint ; the Codger makes to follow, but Foorawn catches his coat, and holds him back.*

Porter. I sent the man called Rankin, paintin' the hall, holier an' hardier than any here, barrin' the lady, to fetch what wouldn't come with me. [*He stiffens and becomes alert.*] I feel it comin' ! [*He runs a hand over head, chest, and legs.*] Tremors here, tremors there : I feel him comin' ! [*He listens.*] Nearer. The Saint of the Bookineeno ! [*At a little distance, a steady blast comes from a horn or cornet.*] Hear that ?

[*Reiligan takes his hat off, and, after hesitating, Codger does the same.*

Reiligan [*alert and uneasy*]. Hear what ?

Foorawn ⎫
Porter ⎬ [*together*]. The blast from his buckineeno !

Reiligan [*uneasily*]. I'll go. I've a lot to do elsewhere. You, Foorawn, can safely settle the saint down. I'll go.
[*He makes for the door.*

Codger [*making to follow*]. Me, too.

Foorawn [*pulling him back*]. You stay here with me, Codger.

Porter [*uneasily*]. I'm goin', too. I'm goin' now. He doesn't like me. I unsettle him, an' him me. [*To Foorawn*] There are other things I have to bring from the railway station. I'm off now be the back way, if you don't mind, Miss ?

Foorawn [*pointing to door left*]. That way.

Porter [*going out*]. There's hardly one of these saints that doesn't want to be a conquering hero. Forced to serve this holy jack or that holy jill. Crosses have odd shapes sometimes. We're all staggerin' about among mysteries !

Codger [*uneasily*]. Time is drivin' me on to ninety, Miss, an' it might be a shock if me thoughts provoked blasts from the boocineeno.

Foorawn [*soothingly*]. Have no fear, as long as I'm here. You're not a bad man, Codger, rather a dear, indeed. Ah ! [*Foorawn's exclamation is caused by the appearance of Rankin at the window with the statue, covered with a white cloth, in his arms. He carries it into the room.*] Here, on its pedestal, Mr. Rankin ; softly ; take the cloth off — up ! We welcome thee, Saint Tremolo, to our home ! Make us worthy of you ; pray for us all, an' help dear Codger to be a good man. [*They lift the cover cautiously from the statue when they have placed it on its pedestal. The statue is a big one, about three feet high, and its form takes the shape of a modern sculpture and somewhat fantastic. The body is barrel-like, the legs are short and fat, the head tiny, and all is dressed in the uniform of a Roman Legionary. The one ecclesiastical sign the figure has is his red-hair tonsure. The horn or buccina is of silver or polished brass, and is coiled round the body, the bell flowing over the right shoulder. They look at it for a moment or two, Rankin and Foorawn close up, the Codger at a distance.*]

Foorawn. It was sin that weighed the railway porter down, and not the statue, for it's quite light, an' all holla underneath.

Codger [*surprise in his voice and some doubt*]. Holla ? A holla statue ; a holla saint. All Hollas Eve — me mind's wanderin'.

Foorawn [*to Rankin*]. And how does the town look, Mr. Rankin ?

Rankin [*enthusiastically*]. Never seen it lovelier ! The whole town's a flapping of flags, an' coloured streamers everywhere, with a great arch of paper flowers at the cross-roads whose centre is a golden mitre and crossed keys of silver ; an' a tall, white candle stands up in every window.

Foorawn. Hear that, Codger ? We've got them all — mitre an' keys for our Bishop of Bishops, roses for our Lady, an' candles for God ! Clap hands, clap hands, till our Bishop comes home ! [*She slaps Rankin on the back vigorously*] Clap hands, you ! [*He does so timidly.*] Clap hands, Codger ! [*She slaps him on the back vigorously.*] Clap hands, all ! [*The Codger claps briskly.*] Hundreds of little fires from the candles an' one great blaze from the bonfire ! Clap hands !

Codger [*losing control of himself*]. Yis, yis, Miss ! [*He blows a wild kiss towards the window.*] We'll flip a kiss to the candles [*he whirls round in a dance*], an' dance a ring round the bonfire !

Foorawn [*restraining him*]. Codger, Codger, please ! What would me Da say if he came in, an' saw you jig-actin' in th' Bishop's room ! An' no kissin' to candles, an' no dancin' round th' bonfire either ; no, nor no annoyin' of th' air or the Bishop's ears with any of your titterin' songs. [*To Rankin*] You go, now, an' help with the buildin' of th' bonfire. [*To the Codger as Rankin goes*] Help me take the sheets from the carpet an' off th' furniture so's to be ready when Keelin comes to polish it all up.

Codger. Lovely carpet, Miss ; no sulkiness in it under a footfall. An archangel could trot across it in his bare feet without feelin' a sting.

Foorawn. Not a bit too good for the good Bishop, though you near ruined it with cement when you fell be th' window.

Codger [*bitterly*]. Some lousy bum shoved me in the wrong direction, Miss.

Foorawn [*helping him and showing him how to fold the sheets neatly*]. Stretch it out. Now fold in two. No more coarse talk, Codger. Now come to meet me so's to fold again — that's it ! Yes, Ballyoonagh will have a new lease of spiritual life ; and you must help, Codger. No more drinking.

Codger [*tonelessly*]. I must give up the drinkin'.

Foorawn [*firmly*]. Smoking, too.

Codger. Smoking, too.

Foorawn. An' senseless singin' as well, Codger. Fold in two. Now come to me — that's it.

Codger [*dubiously*]. I don't know how I'm goin' to give up the singin' ; I've been singin' all me life. After all, Miss, the birds sing, the angels sing, an' I don't see why the poor oul' Codger shouldn't sing too.

Foorawn [*firmly*]. You're neither bird nor angel, Codger, but only a poor old man on his way to th' tomb. God forbid we'd lose you, but, then, we're all steppin' our way to th' tomb.

Codger. We are, we are ; goose-steppin' it, right enough, Miss.

Foorawn [*gaily*]. Goose-steppin' it there, Codger ; yis, an'
lively, too — quick march, man !
   [*She links her arm in his, and they go goose-stepping round
   the room.*

Codger [*hilariously*]. Step be step ! Steady ordher ; left
right, left right ; march on, march on !

Foorawn [*gaily*]. To th' tomb !

Codger [*gaily lilting the Marseillaise*]. Lal de lal lal lal da
dee, lal da lal lal da dee ; march on, march on !
   [*A wailing blast comes from the bookineeno. Foorawn
   hears it, stops her steps in a flash, pulls her arm from
   the Codger's, and starts away from him in a frightened
   manner. The Codger stops, too, astonished, a leg cocked
   up in the air, staying there for a few moments, before he
   slowly lets it down again.*

Foorawn [*angry and frightened*]. Stop this nonsense ; stop
it, fool ! Didn't you hear ?

Codger [*puzzled*]. Hear it ? Hear what, Miss ?

Foorawn [*peevishly*]. No, you didn't hear ; you weren't
listenin'. Oh, Codger, you shouldn't, you shouldn't
coax poor souls to places where they don't want to go ;
to sayin' things that shouldn't be done ; to doin'
things that shouldn't be said. We must fall serious,
so that every step will be a new arrival an' a different
departure.

Codger. A lot in that, oh, a lot, Miss : here we come, an'
there we go.

Foorawn [*solemnly*]. But listen, Codger : If we want to
go from where we think we are, we must go to where
we can't get ; we must set out early before the dew

declines, before the sun rises, before life's fun starts ; always remembering that joy, within the light or under the darkness, is joy under the frock of death.

Codger [trying to be fervent]. Yis. How right you are ! You're right there, right enough ! Couldn't be righter.

Foorawn [helping to take cover off piano, or to fold a sheet]. Now, the last one. Take them all to the lumber-room. The last. Sad word, Codger. Maybe this visit will be someone's last chance. The song sung is the song unheard, the song unsung. The song unsung is the song heard, the song sung.

Codger [enthusiastic]. You're right there, Miss ! [In a half-reverie]. How true an' terrifyin' is all you're after sayin', Miss : enough to make this bugle here hum till it's hot — for years ; yis, for years to come ! [Looking at statue. He touches it, and immediately two short, sharp blasts from the bookineeno are heard. He jumps back, startled.] Jasus ! He doesn't like me either ! Hear them two venomous blasts ! He doesn't want me here. I'd better go.

Foorawn [startled, too, and irritated]. Why did you touch it ? Better go, quick as you can. [She places bundle of linen in his arms] There — off you go ! [She opens the door for the Codger carrying the bundle of linen, and near hidden by it. He goes out. Foorawn crosses to the other door, opens it, looks out to call Keelin. Calling] All ready, Keelin, to come and polish away !
  [She crosses then to the other door, and follows the Codger
  as Keelin enters by the door opposite, followed by Daniel,
  both of them carrying chamois dusters in their hands.
  [As Daniel is polishing the table at one end and Keelin
  at the other, the Railway Porter appears at the window

carrying an inlaid and gaudily decorated stand desk. He calls to them.

Porter [*calling out*]. Eh, there ! [*He turns his back to them on the threshold of the window.*] Take this thing off me spine. Hall full of pots an' ladders, so had to come here. [*As they take it off his back*] That desk's called a Buhl : a piece you won't see every day in the best of places, an' never in Ballyoonagh ; not till now. It's for the Bishop's bedroom. [*Indicating statue of Tremolo — in a whisper*] I see you have the Bookineeno boyo safely bedded.

Keelin. Yis. Isn't the Buhl lovely !

Porter. Decked out with rare mother o' pearl patterns, here an' there, bits of enamelled metals, fancifully turned, this one blue, that one green — be God, he should be able to write a lovely pastoral with a thing like that under his pen !

Keelin [*to Daniel*]. Help me carry it out of the way, Dan, into the hall.
　　[*They carry it across the room to the door on the left, pass out into the hall, leave the desk there, and return to the room.*

Porter [*as they are carrying desk out*]. Wait till yous see the chair I have in the van for yous. I'll get it now. Don't be talkin' !
　　　　　　　　　　　　[*He goes off to get the chair.*

Keelin [*as they come back to the room*]. A chair, too, for the Bishop. Sure, he'll be goin' from one glory to another in this house. I hope his bonfire an' his blessin' will do us some good.

Daniel [*gleefully*]. It's done good be throwin' us together more, anyhow. I've been able to come into the house ; able to see you alone, like now ; an' able to put me arm around your waist like this.
> [*He puts an arm around her.*

Keelin [*snobbily, though no way displeased that his arm's around her*]. Don't forget, Daniel, I'm a lady, that me Da's a Count, an' gave me a high convent education, an' that we live in a grand house, while the Clooncoohys sheltered under a slate roof for the first time, me Da says, when Rural Authorities built them a council house outa the ratepayers' money.

Daniel [*undaunted, knowing that Keelin loves him*]. What's it matter whether a man's born under turrets or under a thatch ? It's the man with the gay heart that rides the waters an' the winds ; who shakes life be the hand when life looks fair, an' shakes her be the shoulder when she shows a frown.

Keelin [*pushing his arms from her waist*]. He's comin' back.
> [*The Porter comes to the window carrying the chair, a gorgeous, slim armchair, all crimson rep, with gilded framework and legs. The crimson back is ornamented with fleurs de lis surmounted by a silver crown.*

Porter. Here 'tis, half throne, half chair, curvin' nicely in the seat to suit the Bishop's backside. Bill Mullarkey, won't you please come home. Looks like this place'll be his heart's first home !

Keelin. Bring it in, please.
> [*The Porter carries it in over the window's threshold, but as soon as he has stepped into the room, three short, sharp blasts come from the cornet, or horn. He drops the chair, and hurries out by the window again.*

Porter [*agitatedly*]. Didja hear that? Has it in for me, that laddo.

Keelin [*surprised*]. Hear what? What ails you?

Porter [*wiping sweat from his forehead*]. Are yous deaf? Didn't yous hear the blasts from the boyo's buckineeno? The minute I set a foot into the room. [*He takes a docket from his pocket and offers it to Keelin*] Here, sign for desk an' chair, an' let me be off while I'm safe. [*Keelin takes the docket, goes to the end of the table where pen and ink are, signs it, and gives it back to the Porter. With a sigh of relief*] Thanks. [*He catches Dan by an arm, and draws him closer*] Listen, me poor boy. [*He catches Keelin by an arm, and draws her closer*] Listen, me poor girl. Listen both, cautiously: Yous have a larboard watch ahoy laddo in this distracted house. Keep a kee veev over your thinkin'. When you talk of this an' not of that, let your voices be as low as a murmurin' wind among the willows. Listen both: never let a single thing yous say about a certain party rise above the surface of a whisper. Hush! Goodbye, poor girl; poor boy, goodbye!

> [*He steals away on tiptoe, and Keelin stands thoughtfully for a moment. Daniel comes over to her, and puts an arm round her.*

Keelin. Oh, Dan, I don't know, I don't know; our love has many enemies.

Daniel [*puzzled*]. Enemies? What are you talking about? There's only your Da.

Keelin [*indicating the statue*]. There's this; there's the Canon; there's all of your own class who are envious of you; and there's my own dark pride warning me against marrying beneath me.

Daniel [*huffily*]. Oh, well, if you think that, let's say goodbye.

Keelin [*sharply*]. Don't be a fool, Dan ! You know it was dinned into me since I was a toddler. You mustn't play with those children, dear ; they aren't fit for you. Then by the nuns, telling me I was a lady, and mustn't do anything unladylike. I can't get rid of the feelin' at the first go.

Daniel [*ardently*]. Let your love falsify your own feelin', Keelin, an' leave me to deal with the Count, your Da, the Canon, an' the town !

Keelin [*doubtfully*]. Oh, don't try to be too brave, too sudden, Dan. It won't be easy, it won't be easy.

Daniel [*confident*]. Just you wait. We're not goin' to let ourselves die in the gloom of Ballyoonagh.

Keelin. Oh, Dan, there's gloom in the outside world as well as in little Ballyoonagh.

Daniel. Sure, I know. I've travelled England an' a bit of Scotland, and found gloom dulling the life of Scot an' Briton. But, here and there, torches flamed in the gloom lighting a way out of it, while here we have to praise an' worship the gloom that stifles us. In the world outside, we would find hours like them we knew as children, when climbing a tree we made the branches merry steps away from childhood's hardship, when we thought the rustling of leaves the lesser lilt of life, and when the stars above were nothing less than our own thoughts gleaming.

Keelin. If the world outside's so good, why did you come back to Ballyoonagh ?

Daniel [*fervently holding her in his arms*]. I came back because you were here.

Keelin. No, Danny, no !

Daniel. Yes, Keelin, yes. Down in foundation, up among the girders, the figure and face of Keelin were always beside me.
   [*Father Boheroe appears at the window, a tired look in his soft eyes, a half-sad, half-amused smile crinkling his sensitive mouth. He stands just outside watching the couple.*

Keelin [*half struggling to free herself, but finally nestling down within Dan's arms*]. No, Danny, no !

Daniel [*bending his head down to her upturned face*]. Yes, Keelin, yes !

Keelin. You mustn't, Danny ; you really mustn't.

Daniel. Mustn't what ?

Keelin. Mustn't say such things ; and you mustn't kiss me.

Daniel [*kissing her several times*]. I know I mustn't ! Oh, Keelin, if we could only stay like this for ever !

Keelin. Life couldn't let us stay together like this for ever, Dan, dear. It wouldn't be good for us ; but if we be constant an' brave, we might be together like this for a long, long time.

Father Boheroe. For a long, long time. [*With mock seriousness*] Aha, I've caught the pair of you.
   [*The couple break away from each other, and stand embarrassed, then go back to the table polishing, Keelin at one end, and Daniel at the other.*

Daniel [*confused and penitent*]. Excuse me, Father, I forgot meself. I shouldn't have done it. I wasn't thinkin'.

Keelin. You didn't forget yourself, Dan. You done what I wanted you to do. You were thinkin' an' there was no harm in the delight of the kisses you gave me !

Father Boheroe. Keelin is right. No need to be penitent, Danny ; a man in a woman's arms may indeed be close to God.

Daniel [*shocked*]. Oh, Father, such a thing to say ! I forget at times that Miss Keelin here's so far above me in her bringin' up, an' that her father's a Count now, a big man an' the right-hand man of Canon Burren. Who am I to think of his daughter ?

Keelin [*pathetically*]. There's all that against us, Father. Oh, what can we do ? We can't go on ; we can't go on.

Father Boheroe [*in a loud and imperative voice — suddenly*]. Listen !
   [*Daniel and Keelin stand intent, listening, for a few moments.*

Keelin [*in an awestruck whisper*]. What is it, Father ; what is it ?

Father Boheroe. I heard God laughing, Keelin.

Keelin [*shocked*]. God laughing ? Oh, Father, how could God laugh ?

Father Boheroe. He's laughing now, Keelin. What else can He do, except destroy the lot of us ?

Daniel [*solemnly*]. Laughing at what, Father ?

Father Boheroe. Laughing at the punch and judy show of Ballyoonagh, at you, Keelin, for thinking your Da governs your soul and body ; at you, Danny, for giving Count Reiligan a higher place than God might give him. Laughing at me, too. Oh, who are you to dream today of a greater tomorrow ! Who am I to dream of it either !

Keelin. It's nice to dream, an' it does us good ; but when we come out of our dream, we daren't think of what it told us.

Father Boheroe. Well, my children, if you daren't think of what your dream has told you, remember the bonfire, the things for the Bishop's comfort ; see you do your duty well. [*To Daniel*] Give up Keelin. [*To Keelin*] Give up Dan. Good-bye to you both.
> [*He goes towards the window.*

Keelin [*convulsively clutching Daniel's arm*]. No, no ; I won't give Danny up ! I'm not frightened, Father, not a bit frightened.

Daniel [*putting his arm round her*]. Nor am I frightened ! I refuse to be frightened ! If the future gives us a gay gown, we'll wear it, an' be glad ; if the future weaves us one of mourning, we'll wear it, too, an' go on bravely wherever life may lead us !

Keelin [*softly — looking up at Daniel*]. Wherever life may lead us, we go together.

Daniel [*looking down at her*]. Together !

Father Boheroe [*delightedly — half dancing towards the piano*]. That's the stuff, children ! You are both now in the fierce flow of what the poets have glorified in a thousand songs. Through time and through eternity, you will never feel quite the same glad glow again. [*He plays the soft notes of a waltz very softly on the piano.*] Get to yourselves the courage to last it out. You've escaped from the dominion of the big house with the lion and unicorn on its front ; don't let yourselves sink beneath the meaner dominion of the big shop with the cross and shamrock on its gable. Whatever comes, refuse to be frightened, and take whatever the glow may bring, be it the mourning habit or the golden gown !

Keelin ⎫
Daniel ⎭ [*together*]. The mourning habit or the golden gown !

Father Boheroe [*playing in a more lively way*]. Grand ! Boot and saddle and away ! Blue bonnets, blue bonnets over the border !

Keelin ⎫
Daniel ⎭ [*together*]. Blue bonnets over the border !

[*Keelin and Daniel have come into the rhythm of the music, and now, close together, with their arms around each other, they move quietly and dreamily about the room in front of the table. When they are well under the music's spell, the door on the right flies open, and in comes the Count, excited, and with a look of fury on his face ; he is followed by the Canon, now Monsignor, whose face carries on it a look of angry exasperation.*

[*Daniel pulls wildly away from Keelin's hold, which he succeeds in doing, though she holds him tightly to her for a few moments.*

[*Daniel retreats backwards before the angry glare from the Count. Father Boheroe continues to play the piano, but very softly now.*

Reiligan [*furiously*]. What's this? [*He rushes over to Daniel, grips him by the shoulders, and shakes him.*] Who told you to do a belly-to-belly dance with me lady daughter? God in heaven, the like of you, you dung-scented menial, to wind your arms around a lady!

Daniel [*frightened*]. I didn't mean it, I didn't really. I musta been mad, sir.

Reiligan [*as furiously as ever*]. Get outa me house, outa me employment, outa me sight!

Father Boheroe [*rather loudly*]. Blue bonnets are over the border!

Keelin [*running over and catching Daniel's arm*]. We love each other! I won't let you, won't let anyone, take Dan away from me!

Daniel [*roughly forcing her hand from his arm*]. For God's sake, girl, have sense, an' don't make things worse!

Reiligan [*gripping Keelin roughly, swinging her around, and giving her a pushing fling that sends her, almost spinning, to the other end of the room where she subsides into the half throne, half chair*]. Disgrace to your father, disgrace to your sister, you jade, shameless an' shockin'! I'll deal with you later.

Father Boheroe [*going over to where Keelin sits, almost silently sobbing on the chair, and laying a gentle hand on her shoulder*]. You are a liar, Reiligan, regarding your daughter. She is a disgrace to no truth, to no virtue.

Reiligan [*wrathfully*]. You encouraged them, did you, Father Boheroe?

Father Boheroe [*quietly but firmly*]. I gave them my blessing, and left another hovering over all they intended to do.

Reiligan. It's not for me to say you scatter your blessin's curiously, Father Boheroe. I'll leave all that to the Right Rev. Monsignor Burren.

Canon [*after a pause — to Daniel*]. Go now, Clooncoohy, and help with the Bishop's Bonfire ; and, tomorrow, come at nine o'clock to the Presbytery — I must have a talk with you.

Daniel [*submissively*]. Yis, Canon.

Reiligan [*explosively*]. Monsignor, you lug ! Our Canon's a Mor..ignor, now.

Daniel [*apologetically*]. I'm very sorry, Canon, I didn't know.

Canon [*unceremoniously pushing him out by the door — impatiently*]. Oh, go on, man ! [*To Reiligan*] Clooncoohy won't offend again. Come, Count, we must have a talk. [*As Reiligan steps aside to allow the Canon to go out first*] No ; you first, my dear man.
    [*The Count goes out while the Canon pauses by the door.*

Reiligan [*as he is going out — to Father Boheroe*]. May I say, Father Boheroe, that I'd rather you didn't bang about the piano I've had tuned up and polished bright for the Bishop.

Canon [*quietly to Father Boheroe*]. You're clever, Father — and sincere, I hope — but your cleverness seems only to make persons more unhappy than they were. I'm afraid I cannot commend the way you try to lead my poor people towards illusions. Can't you understand that their dim eyes are able only for a little light ? Damn it, man, can't you see Clooncoohy can never be other than he is ? You're very popular with our people, but remember that the love they may have for you doesn't come near the fear they have for Reiligan [*he pauses*] or the reverence they must show for their Parish Priest.

Father Boheroe [*as quietly as the Canon*]. There's Keelin to think of as well as Clooncoohy, Canon Burren. God help us, Monsignor, for by fear, we have almost lost our love for our neighbour ; even our worship is beginning to have the look of the fool's cap and the sound of the jester's bells.

Canon [*sarcastically*]. I seem to hear the tinny tinkle of the bells in what you say. [*With meaning.*] I think, Father Boheroe, it is near time for you and me to have a friendly chat with our Bishop.
      [*He goes out, shutting the door behind him.*

Father Boheroe [*tenderly — to Keelin*]. My poor child, my poor child.

Keelin [*brokenly*]. What am I to do, Father ; oh, what am I to do ! Dan hadn't the courage to stand up to them. Dan has forsaken me, forsaken me ! I will never marry. I will die as I am ; I love him, an' he's lost to me now !

Father Boheroe. My poor child !
    [*The room suddenly flashes into darkness, a cold wind sweeps through it, and when the light comes again, it comes only to the sad and pensive density of dusk.*

Keelin [*startled — with a sudden shuddering shiver*]. What was that, Father ? [*She clutches his arm.*] A shiver cold and powerful through my body, into my soul.

Father Boheroe [shivering too]. Cold and powerful through my body, into my soul as well.

Keelin [frightened]. What is it ?   What was it, Father ?

Father Boheroe. It was, my child, a long, sad sigh from God.

                         END OF ACT II

Still the drawing-room in Reiligan's house ; all spruced and spiced now for the Bishop's stay there. An electric light, covered with a light-green shade, hangs from the ceiling over the table. Near the fireplace is a standard lamp whose shade is white, and a small stand-lamp on the sideboard is decked out with a yellow shade. There are table-mats on the table ready for any hot plates that may be put there. The brandy in a decanter stands on the sideboard with a bottle of soda-water and another bottle of brandy beside it. It is night-time, and the window stands half open, for the air is very warm, and even a few birds are still twittering in the ash tree.

The Prodical is sitting, very dignified indeed, in a chair by the head of the table. He is dressed in the uniform of a waiter, apron and all. He wears a piece of chamois folded on his head, so as (he thinks) it may look like a mitre.

Daniel is dressed like a waiter, too, though the suit is too baggy for him as Prodical's is too tight, and the trousers a little too short.

Daniel is fussing at the sideboard, evidently pretending to be waiting on the Bishop. He suddenly stands rigid, stiff to attention.

Daniel [*shouting fiercely*]. Silence ! me Lord Bishop, Bill Mullarkey is about to spake !

Prodical [*pompously*]. Dan, me son, take me epicpiscopal advice, an' keep your young innocent puss outa the whiskey-tumbler, out of a bad book, an' keep far from the girls, for a young bitch's enfiladin' blessin' is the devil's choicest curse !

Daniel. Sound christian doctrine, right reverend. Would you like any more soup, your reverence, holy man, benevolent Bishop ?

Prodical. Bring me another glass of brandy, fella.

Daniel. I will that. [*He pours one for Prodical.*] An' one for meself. [*He pours another and fetches it to the Prodical.*] There y'are. [*He goes back to sideboard, lifts the glass, and turns towards the Prodical*] To the Bishop, the Bishop's Bonfire — to hell with the two of them !
  [*Keelin comes into the room carrying a piece of music and a chamois duster in her hand. She passes by Daniel without a look or a word, and goes to the piano, which she opens, and places the music on the rest. The sheet of music shows the title of 'Kiss Me, Kate'. There is a silent pause.*

Prodical [*remonstratively*]. You're gettin' too furious, Dan. We're riskin' what we needn't risk. We're steppin' into where curious things may be whirrin' about. [*Taking the comic mitre from his head*] I don't feel easy trying to make a cod of the Bishop's visit, and the image of St. Tremolo with his eyes out on sticks watchin' us. You'd never know what might happen.
  [*The Codger has appeared at the window carrying a lantern in his hand. He lingers there, watching and listening to those in the room.*

Daniel. Let anything happen ; let everything happen ! I'm a hard case when I'm roused. I'm reckless. [*Bragging to restore his lost reputation with Keelin*] No fear in me of him stickin' his neck out. The whole house is bloomin' with statues. Doesn't matter to me. I won't be long here. When the fun's over, I'm

off. [*Keelin becomes interested, and listens intently.*] I'm
not goin' to stay as a pot-walloper in Ballyoonagh.
Dan Clooncoohy was made for something better. I've
enough saved to keep me a fortnight, so when the
Bishop's Bonfire's blazed its way to black soot and
grey ash, I head for England's shore.

Keelin [*who has stolen nearer and nearer to him as he speaks —
with an intense appeal*]. I've some saved, too, sewn up in
the mattress of me bed ; thirty pounds an' more !
Oh, Danny, take me with you ! The money's all
yours ; I'm all yours — oh, Danny, do !

Daniel [*ignoring her — to Prodical*]. Let's be goin', Prod —
there's more to be done yet.
　　[*Prodical has been going towards the door, and now passes
　　out ; Daniel has been delayed for a moment by Keelin's
　　hold on an arm.*

Keelin [*with anguish in her appeal, as he shakes her hold off, and
follows the Prodical*]. Oh, Danny, do !
　　[*But he goes out without a yea or nay, and quietly shuts
　　the door after him, leaving her standing disconsolate, her
　　breast heaving with silent sobs. After a pause, the Codger
　　comes into the room, leaves his lantern thoughtlessly down
　　on the fresh, grand carpet, and goes over to where she is
　　standing.*

Codger [*gently*]. Me poor little girl, me poor little child !
There's small use of me sayin' you're better without
him. [*He stays silent for a moment, then says vehemently*]
Jasus ! If I was only half me age, I'd gather you up in
me arms, carry you outa th' house, out of th' town,
out th' country to th' nearest port, where you could
live with a few bits of furniture, a bright fire, an'
geraniums in the window !

Keelin [*brokenly*]. Oh, Codger, I'm to be pitied, for Danny's nigh broken me heart ! I was ready to defy them all.

Codger [*viciously*]. An' they tell me there's a statue of Ireland's hero, Cuchullain, somewhere up in Dublin. [*Pathetically*] Oh, Keelin, Keelin me darling, I'm Irish an' ashamed of it.

Keelin [*suddenly putting her arms round the Codger, and kissing him on the cheek*]. Oh, Codger, dear Codger, I wish to God that you were me Da !
    [*The clang of an opening and shutting gate is heard in the garden.*

Codger [*stroking Keelin's hair*]. Me poor child ; we'll talk again when things are quieter ; talk a lot. There's someone comin' now.
    [*They separate ; Keelin going to the piano which she starts polishing ; the Codger to the lantern on the carpet, as the Canon — now Monsignor — appears at the window, and comes into the room.*

Canon [*seeing the lantern*]. Ah, a dirty lantern on the good carpet ! Slap it down — anywhere will do ! Clumsy, thoughtless fellow ! Why isn't it alight in the garden to give a glimpse of gate and pathway ?

Codger [*brusquely*]. No oil ; goin' to get some now, Canon.

Canon [*testily*]. Monsignor, my man ; 'tis Monsignor now.

Codger [*shortly*]. I know ; but you'll always be the Canon to me.

Canon. Something even less than a Canon to him. [*To Keelin*] Surly, disrespectful old man, the Codger. Don't listen too leniently, Keelin, to that old rascal's gab. Well, still busy, my child.

Keelin. Yes, Monsignor — as you can see.

Canon [*graciously*]. I was just talking to the Bishop's brother, Farmer Mullarkey : a good man, young and active lad.

Keelin. Hardly a lad ; why, he's well over fifty, Father.

Canon [*testily*]. That's not considered old these days. He was asking about you, Keelin. [*A pause.*] A strong farmer, and anxious to settle down : to marry. He likes you, my daughter, and a girl could go further and fare worse for a husband.

Keelin [*facing the Canon*]. He doesn't care a damn about me ! He's in debt to me Da, and him an' me Da want to join their property.

Canon [*with decision*]. And a very sensible thing to do, child. You should think about it. Two hundred acres of good land, thirty head of fine cattle, pigs, and poultry ; fine crops of wheat, and barley, a commodious barn, nearly new, and green pastures for many more animals. Joined to you in the holy Sacrament of Matrimony, my daughter, the son-in-law of the Count and the brother of the Bishop would be next in power to the Count himself ; and, when the Count goes, as we all must go one day, you and he would lead the day-to-day life of Ballyoonagh.

 [*Reiligan appears opposite to the door near which Keelin is standing, facing the Monsignor, who is standing at the window side of the table, with a hand resting on the head of St. Tremolo. Reiligan is in the full uniform of a Papal Count — short jacket, long trousers, braided cuffs and collar, elegant sword, feathered cocked hat, and all. Keelin ignores him, keeping her look fixed towards the Monsignor.*

Keelin [*passionately*]. I don't want his acres of good land,
I don't want his fine cattle, his crops of wheat an'
barley, his pigs or his poultry, his long an' lofty barn,
or his grassy-green fields either ! [*She goes to the door,
opens it, ready to go out, turning back to stare straight again
at the Monsignor.*] I don't want old grey-headed Paul
Mullarkey, with or without the Sacrament of Matrimony. [*In a passionate shout*] I want me Danny !
          [*She goes wildly out, banging the door hard after her.*

Reiligan [*furiously*]. There's a convent-educated girl for
you — the rebellious little bitch ! Wants her Danny,
does she ? Be God, whatever happens, she won't get
her Danny !

Canon [*soothingly*]. No, no, Count, she won't get her
Danny. And, now, Michael, be patient. She is very
young, and she believes she has suffered a great loss.
Time will tell her differently. What she thinks is love
will soon be but a thought in the darkness, fainting into
nothingness in the daylight of commoner feeling. It
is a common thing for the young to think that their
way is wiser and brighter than God's way.

Reiligan. Last thing they think of now is God's way.
Mullarkey himself doesn't help much. For a man of
fifty-eight, he should be ashamed of himself, tellin'
me once he'd as lief have his pipe beside him as any
woman. If it wasn't for the hold I've over him he
wouldn't look over a hedge at Keelin.

Canon. He'll soon be glad to come into the house,
Michael, so don't worry. Let Keelin be for the time
being. Her Danny won't bother you again — I've
made sure of that ; he saw the error of his way.

Reiligan. A real lady livin' with a lout ! I can't get the meanin' of them even thinkin' they could ever come together.

Canon. Well, don't try to get the meaning. Even the Book God is writing will have very little meaning for us till it's finished.

Codger [*heard calling from the garden*]. Think of what you're doin', think of what you're doin', man !
   [*The Prodical comes to the window, followed by the Codger, who stands a little way from the window in the garden. Prodical comes into the room. He is excited and a look of tense determination sours his face. He is a little breathless.*

Reiligan [*irritably — to Prodical*]. Well, what d'ye want, what d'ye want now ?

Prodical [*pushing him carelessly aside*]. Not you, not you — Monsignor. [*To the Canon*] Heard you were here, an' hurried here to catch you. Afraid I'd miss you. I must get rid of it. I'm lost if I don't ; must shove it outa sight, outa me mind. I'm lost if I don't.

Codger [*loudly — from near the window — to Prodical*]. You're lost, too, if you do. Better, be far, man, to be lost with it than to be lost without it !

Canon [*impatiently — to Prodical*]. Well, what is it, what is it you want ? Get rid of what ?

Prodical [*to the Canon*]. Wait a minute, you ! [*To the Codger*] Go away ; I won't listen to you. You're a menace to me.

Codger [*loudly — to the Prodical*]. An hour after it's done, you'll be comin' to ask me why did I let you do it.

Canon [*indignantly — to Codger*]. Go away, and let Carranaun speak. [*To Prodical*] Now, my son, what is it?

Codger [*ignoring the Canon — to Prodical*]. You sorrow before you do anything, an' you sorrow when it's done. You're puttin' years on yourself with your perpetual sorrowin'!

Prodical [*out to the Codger*]. I'm not sorrowin' now. I'm full of elation at me own resolution not to be beaten be a bottle. For the time bein', Codger, you're just Satan tryin' to wheedle me into sin.

Codger. You're wheedlin' yourself, Prodical; you're wheedlin' yourself into a right disaster.

Canon [*testily — to Prodical*]. What's wrong? What are you trying to wheedle yourself from, man?

Prodical [*ignoring Canon — to the Codger*]. You're bad company. You're always imposin' yourself in the way of me vow.

Reiligan [*angrily — to Prodical*]. Monsignor Burren's askin' you a question, man.

Prodical [*loudly and angrily*]. Let him wait a minute! [*To the Codger*] A minute after makin' a resolution, I always find you in front of me, or hear you hailin' me from behind. You're my menacin' ubique. You may well take it easy, for you don't sorrow as I sorrow. You bury your sorrows in a song, while my sorrowin's like the moanin' of the harbour bar on a misty an' a mournful night.

Codger [*vehemently — to the Prodical*]. Can't you give it to me, an' I'll dispose of it for you? Don't sully a comrade's love with the test of a sour behaviour. You'll **never see it** again till it's dead.

Canon [*shaking Prodical's left arm*]. Dispose of what, my son?

Reiligan [*shaking his right arm*]. Till what's dead?

Codger [*to Reiligan and Canon*]. Oh, shut it, will yous, for a minute? [*To the Prodical*] Mind you, you'll live to be sorry for your wild notion. Let me take care of it.

Prodical [*decisively*]. I will not. I'm not goin' to furnish you with the means of committin' a sin I'm tryin' to escape meself.

Canon [*impatiently shaking the Prodical's arm*]. What is all this about, man? I and the Count have things to discuss, and can't wait here all night — what is it!

Prodical [*after rummaging in his tail-pocket and taking out a pint bottle of whiskey, which he displays to all in the room*]. This is what it's all about. I've taken a vow never for ever to drink again; an', to make sure, an' rid meself of temptation, I want you, kind Monsignor, to present this bottle of danger to the sacred St. Tremolo standin' there in the table's middle, appealin' to men to be sensible and be sober.

Codger [*appealingly — to Prodical*]. Throw it to me, Prodical. Be sensible even at the eleventh hour — throw it to me!

Canon [*graciously*]. St. Tremolo's always on the watch to warn, and, when his warning's heard, is always ready to help. Besides, we mustn't have any nonsense during the Bishop's visit. Give me the bottle.

Prodical [*earnestly — but hesitating to give the bottle*]. We're all part of the Bishop's Bonfire, flaming up with feelin's of welcomin' good-will. I wouldn't like the Bishop to notice me noddin'.

Codger [*sarcastically*]. It might do the Right Reverend a lot of good to see a part of the real life in the town he comes to bless !

Canon [*angrily — to the Codger*]. Be off, you mischievous poacher on men's desire to do good deeds ! You wicked man ! I warn you the time is near at hand when the cold clay of death will fill that vicious mouth of yours. [*To Reiligan*] Oh, Count, break your silence into a reprimand.

Reiligan [*shouting at the Codger*]. Take yourself off ! What are you doing here, anyway ?

Codger. Been cleanin' out your *de profundis* urn, an' am waitin' to be told whereabouts in the garden I'm to put the lighted lantern.

Reiligan [*angrily*]. On the bricks, mouth ; on the top of the bricks ! Do it, an' be off !

Canon [*amiably — to the Prodical*]. Give me the bottle, my son. [*Prodical hands him the bottle, and the Canon lifts the statue, and puts the bottle into the hollow under the legs and cloak of the figure. Putting the bottle away.*] In you go ! You are out of season, now you are out of sight and out of mind.

Prodical [*firmly*]. Out of sight an' mind, wha' ? Yis.

Canon [*patting Prodical between the shoulders*]. Your temptation's imprisoned in a holy place, now ; and you are free.

Prodical [*with dubious assurance*]. Free, Canon, wha' ? Yis, free !

Codger [*shouting from without the window*]. No !

Canon [*patting Prodical's shoulder*]. And safe, my son.

Prodical [*somewhat dubiously*]. Safe, too.

Codger [*shouting from outside*]. No !

Prodical [*shouting out to the Codger*]. Yis !

Codger [*who hasn't stirred from the window — dismally*]. They've got you now where they want you, Prodical. What'll you do when the band plays, the people cheer, the bonfire blazes, an' the Bishop comes waltzin' into the town, an' you with a dry tongue in a dusty mouth, parched, an' powerless to feel anything but a desire for a *domine vobiscum* death.
[*He leaves the window, lantern in hand, and goes over to the pile of bricks to fix it there.*]

Reiligan [*suddenly listening intently*]. Whist ! Is that them ? No, not yet. [*To the Monsignor*] The cattle, Father. [*Looks at his wrist-watch.*] Jerry the cowman should have had them home more than an hour ago. I'm anxious. Left them to gawk at the flags in the town, maybe. Rushin' to see the flags, rushin' to hear the band practisin', rushin' to see the bonfire, regardless of the cattle ! [*Shouting to the Codger*] Eh, you, slip down along the road, an' see can you see any sign of Jerry with the cows ! [*He listens again. The sound of the lowing of cattle is heard, faintly at first, then louder as they come nearer to the house, then fading away as they pass on their way to the byres. He runs to the window and shouts to the Codger.*] It's all right, Codger — they're here ! [*He peers out into the garden.*] Oh, he's gone now ! He'll go clamping down the road now ; *he'll* have a look at the Bishop's Bonfire ; he'll stop to listen to the band practising ; he'll be everywhere but where he's wanted !

[*To the Prodical*] After him, you, an' bring him back before he gets to tavern or town.

Prodical [*with dismay*]. Me, is it? What the hell d'ye think I am? A fine sight I'd look gallopin' down the road in these garments! I feel bad enough sequestered in a sequestered house, without runnin' out to show meself under the public stare of the stars. Send someone commonly accoutred to do your biddin'.

Reiligan [*shouting*]. Where're the others, where're the others to send!

Prodical [*shouting just as loud*]. How the hell do I know?

Canon. Boys, boys! [*Laying a friendly hand on Prodical's arm*] We must all leave off shouting, for it would distress the Bishop if he heard us shouting at each other. Besides, you look very attractive in the suit that's to be worn while helping to serve the Bishop's meals. [*Soothing Reiligan with a pat on the arm*] Take it easier, Count; try to take it easier. It's trying, very, but we must be calm: no shouting, please.

Reiligan [*furiously*]. I'll hunt some of them out! [*He makes for the door on the right, and, as he reaches it, a tremendous kicking is heard on the door to the left. Turning back in anguish*] Oh, who's kicking all the good paint off the newly painted door? [*He rushes to it, pulls it open, and Rankin staggers in, carrying a tall palm in a tub, painted with circular bars of yellow and white. Furiously — to Rankin*] You jelly-brained eejut, what d'ye mean kickin' a newly painted door to pieces? [*He notices that Rankin is wearing boots.*] Oh, looka the boots he's wearin'! [*He runs to the door and examines it.*] Looka, the paint's scattered, an' even the wood is bruised. Look at it, look at it!

Rankin [*who has placed the palm on the near end of the table, and has come over a little way to glance at the door*]. It isn't much. I had to get it open someway. A little lick of paint an' it'll look as well as ever.

Reiligan [*fiercely*]. What're you wearin' your boots for? Where's the slippers I gave you? Where's your slippers, where's your slippers?

Rankin [*gloomily*]. They're in the back pocket of me tailed-coat, if you want to know. They were cuttin' the feet off me.

Reiligan. Let them, then. You're not to cross this room again without your slippers on you. [*He now notices that the palm is standing on the table.*] Ooh! Looka where he put the palm! [*He grips hold of Rankin and forces him to the palm and the tub.*] Borin' right down into the polished wood of me table! Take it off, take it off, take it off!

Rankin [*protestingly — dragging the tub into his arms*]. I had to lay it somewhere!

Reiligan. Don't drag, don't drag it, man! The table! [*When Rankin has the tub in his arms.*] Oh, looka, looka the table! Junks out of it!

Rankin [*plaintively*]. Open the door here, open the door.

Canon [*shouting*]. Get out of our sight!

Rankin [*less plaintively*]. Open this door, then, or this palm'll be plungin' about on the carpet!

Reiligan [*hastening to the door, opening it, and pushing Rankin out*]. Go on, get out, you Jezebel's get! and put the slippers on. [*To the Prodical*] You go, Prodical, get a chamois duster, and try to get these scratches out of

the table. And get Rankin to put his lick of paint on
the bruised door, an' make sure he puts the palm in the
porch outside the front door.

[*Prodical goes out.*

Canon. Careless fools. They have me heart-scalded,
Count. No regard for anything : see a window-pane
cracked — push it in ! See a banister loose — pull it
out !

Reiligan. They'll make everything unfit for the Bishop
by the time they're done doin' violence to them. [*He
comes to the table and bends over the list on it.*] Almost
everything at hand now. Manus has forgotten nothing.
Let me see. Four hot-water bottles haven't come yet,
an' the rug to go by the Bishop's bed. Yes, an' the
wine. That isn't ticked off either. [*A kicking by a
heavy boot, harder than that done by Rankin, is heard again
on the door to the left.*] Good God ! Again ! The
door'll be down ! [*He rushes over to it, and Daniel
staggers into the room, carrying a palm in a tub similar to the
one already borne in by Rankin. Madly*] Looka the door
again ! In another spot too ! The whole panel's
pattered and battered.

Daniel [*staggering, gives a complete turn, glances at the door,
and wheels again to go on his journey*]. Oh, that ? A little
lick of paint'll put that right.

[*He wheels round in a circle to turn and answer Reiligan,
the palm held at a right angle, a left angle, as he struggles
to keep it upright.*

Canon [*shouting*]. Careful, you fool !

Reiligan [*moaningly*]. Another lick of paint ! They'll
never be satisfied. They're distillin' destruction all

over the place ! [*Daniel, when he comes near to the door on the right, planks the palm on the end of the table nearest to it, and goes to the door to open it for himself, as Reiligan turns, and sees him do it. Frantically*] Aw, the table ! Tear that too !

Daniel [*as he goes staggering out*]. It's nothin'. You can put a plate over it or somethin'.

Reiligan [*sinking into a chair*]. A plate over it or somethin' ! Aw, what's the use of the Bishop comin' ? What's the use of tryin' to bring a little culture into the town ? It only adds to a body's sorra !

Codger [*heard singing outside in the garden*]:
  The rose that is fresh in the vase today
  Will be flung away, fadin', tomorrow ;
  An' ev'ry song sung be a singer gay
  Has in it the seed of a sorra.
[*Appearing at the window, looking into the room, and speaking to Reiligan*] Will I light the lantern now ?

Reiligan [*testily*]. Light it, light it, an' be damned to you !

Codger [*going back into the garden*]. Righto. [*He sings again :*]
  Go away, get away, sorra, go !
  No foot hastens forward to meet thee ;
  Come in the midnight or come at cock-crow,
  No hand will be stretch'd out to greet thee !
[*Codger lights the lantern. The red panel of glass is towards the window, so that it looks like a red eye watching those in the room. The other panels, white glass, shine out and show dimly the gateway, the wall, maybe the urn, and, maybe, parts of the elegant, branching ash tree, looking dark now from the window-view.*

Canon [*bitterly*]. Listen to him ! You'd think butter wouldn't melt in his mouth. I often wonder, Reiligan, why you keep that vicious-mouthed old man in your employment.

Reiligan. Well, Monsignor, he's the best man in all the country round to trim a rick or thatch one. A clever hand with the scythe, as well as knowing the soil in every field for miles round, what you can sow in this field, and can't in that one. A right good man, too, with the cattle when the cowman's away, and a sheep-shearer still that no one near can match. Clever, too, with hammer, saw, an' chisel at all but first-class work. And he's well over eighty, Father. No ; no one but God can shift the wily old Codger from Ballyoonagh.

Canon. Things belonging to Caesar, Count. Remember there are still the things of God. A favourite of Father Boheroe, too. A fine choice, I must say. Another pet of his is Manus Moanroe, another fine choice.

Reiligan. A gifted fella, too, Father, as clever on the business end of a farm as the Codger is at the hand-work. Pity he isn't a good Catholic. Yes, a gifted man. The Codger, too. Bad Catholics, bad Catholics, but gifted.

Canon [*bitterly*]. The devil's very lavish with his gifts to those who serve him, Michael. [*Briskly*] But we must think of little now but the Bishop's visit. That's what concerns us now, Michael. When that's over, we can talk of the Codger and of Moanroe.

Reiligan [*as briskly — getting on to his feet*]. The Bishop's visit — you're right, Monsignor ; we can't leave any-thing to chance. Now where the hell's that Prodical ? He went out for a chamois an hour ago, and he isn't back. Listening, I suppose, to Dan telling him how he near battered down oul' Reiligan's door, with the Prodical drinking it all in, to spread it, later on, over the whole town. [*He leans on the table and buries his head in his hands.*] The malicious bastards ! An' all I've done for them ! Like a father to some of them. What would the town be like, if it wasn't for Reiligan ?

Canon [*laying a hand on his shoulder — soothingly*]. The Prefect of our Confraternity mustn't lose courage. When our anxiety and excitement have passed, Michael [*with grimness*], we'll do our best to put the fear of God in them ! They understand only the harsh word and the lash from the whip. The low-minded always envy the successful and the good.

Reiligan [*raising himself from the table*]. Looka, Monsignor, a lot of them would twist themselves into a big laugh if this house fell in on itself while the Bishop was comin' up the pathway. Oh, a venomous bunch, the most of them. [*As the Prodical comes in with the chamois*] Ah, here you are at last. Get to work, man, get to work.

Prodical [*easily*]. All in good time. The four hot-water bottles have come, and the rug, too. An' Foorawn wants someone in the kitchen to pluck plover an' peel potatoes. [*Looking at the table*] It'll take more'n chamois to take these furrows outa the table.

Reiligan [*irritably*]. Oh, try, man, try, before you start cryin'.

Prodical [*indignantly*]. Cryin' ? Who's cryin' ? Nothin' easier than to cover the rents with a plate or somethin'.

Canon [*who has gone to the window, looked out into the garden, and come back again*]. The Codger's not in the garden now. I thought he might be the one who could help in the kitchen.

Foorawn [*appearing at the door*]. Da, send someone down to the kitchen to peel potatoes an' pluck plover. Dan won't go ; says he's no cook's mate.

Reiligan [*to the Canon*]. You see, Father, how they're gettin' outa hand? Any of them who've ever been in England almost expect you to call them Mister now. [*To Foorawn*] Well, search out the Codger.

Foorawn. Oh, I've already asked him : he won't do it either.

Reiligan [*sarcastically*]. An' what did that old gentleman say ?

Foorawn [*uneasily*]. I wouldn't care to say what he said.

Reiligan [*impatiently*]. Go on — out with it, out with it !

Canon [*encouragingly*]. Go on, daughter ; don't be afraid. We can partly guess what the reprobate might say.

Foorawn. He said that if the holy Monsignor plucked the plover, he'd peel the spuds.

Reiligan. An' had me own daughter, devoted to perpetual chastity, nothin' to say to the oul' blasphemer ?

Foorawn. Of course she had : she told him no one would think of expecting holy hands that held holy things should be set to pluck a plover.

Reiligan. An' what did he say to that homer, eh — the infidelian dastard ?

Foorawn [*uneasily*]. No, no. He said somethin' shockin' ; something that frightened me.

Canon. You mustn't be frightened at what such an old rascal would say. We should get to know the full scope of the irreverent ruffian's mind. What did he say, Foorawn ?

Foorawn. He said, Father, that since the holy hands of Christ washed the feet of His Disciples, the half-holy hands of the Canon shouldn't be afraid to peel a spud.

Canon [*firmly*]. You hear, Count ?.

Reiligan. Terrible that such a one should be let go on fermentin' mockin' thoughts of sacred things in the holy quietness of Ballyoonagh !
[*They are all shocked — except the Prodical, who is puzzled — and remain silent. Then the chanting voice of the Codger is heard in the garden again.*]

Codger [*singing in the garden*]:
Ah, where is the laughter rich of children mad at
    play ?
Gone, too, is the lover and his lass
From all the hawthorn's fragrance in the month of
    June or month of May.
Where, where is the time when life had something
    fine to say ?

Canon. Hear him ! [*Jeeringly*] The lover and his lass. What a filthy mind the sly old fool has !
[*Now the Codger is seen before the window, just as Father Boheroe comes into the garden by the gate. He comes over to the Codger who is carrying a branchy, big geranium, topped with many lovely clusters of scarlet flowers. He holds it up for all in the room to see, while Father Boheroe stands beside him.*]

Codger [*holding the geranium forth*]. Here's the geranium for

your urn.   A handsome plant.   Lovelier than the
Count in all his glory, and lovelier than the Monsignor
would be, either, were he dollied up in the scarlet robe
of a cardinal.   God's work, gentlemen an' lady.

Father Boheroe. Helped by man, my friend ; it's a culti-
vated plant.   God and man together.

Codger. Helped be man, right enough.   Man has to
finish what God begins.   Lovely blossoms : red as the
wrath of God ; red as the holy blood of Christ
sprinklin' mercy over all, unknown to some I know
in Ballyoonagh.

Canon [*coldly, but fiercely*]. Go to your own, for you
blaspheme even in your saner sayings.   You make a
contraband of God's mercy, you vicious void in God's
kingdom !

Reiligan [*coming nearer to the window, and facing the Codger*].
Set it in the urn, without more ado, and then go.

Codger [*taken by surprise*]. Go ?   Go where ?

Reiligan. Outa the garden ; outa any property of mine.
I've no more need of you.   Your evil thoughts or your
croakin' voice isn't goin' to be heard any more again
in any place owned be Reiligan.   So off you go !

Foorawn [*agitatedly*]. Oh, no, no !   The Codger's a good
old man : we all love the Codger.

Father Boheroe [*putting a hand on the shoulder of the Codger
furthest from him, so that it looks as if he had an arm around
him*]. Monsignor, Monsignor, we are stripping Joseph
of his coat of many colours again.   Oh, I fear, I fear
we do wrong to diminish the usefulness, or admonish
the honesty, of a brave man.

Codger [*to Father Boheroe*]. Never mind, Father. [*To Reiligan*] Your loss, Count, well as mine. The old age pension'll keep me in bread, tea an' onions, an' what more does an old man want ? In me time, I've fasted far more than the Bishop who's comin', or the Monsignor who's here. I'll set the flower in the urn, for there's no ill-will between me an' the geranium ; then, I'll go.

Canon. Go then, and no more talk.

Prodical. No, no ; the Codger's never goin' to be a stranger in the town of Ballyoonagh. It's a tiring shame !

Foorawn. It's a shame !
　[*Codger goes into the garden, and may be seen putting the plant into the urn.*

Reiligan [*violently*]. Your concern isn't with the Codger. You mind your own work !

Foorawn [*impatiently*]. Who's goin' to do the plover and the potatoes then ?

Reiligan [*as impatiently*]. What about Keelin ? Get Keelin, get Keelin !

Foorawn. Oh, she's in a mood ; won't do anything ; won't bless herself even.
　[*Keelin appears at the door left as Daniel appears at the door right.*

Keelin [*vehemently*]. The Bishop can peel his own spuds !

Daniel [*vehemently*]. The Bishop can pluck his own plover !

Reiligan [*furiously*]. Be off, the two of you ! We don't need yous. We've one here darin' an' dyin' to do both.

[*To Prodical*] You go, oul' son, to the kitchen, an' do
the spuds an' the plover.

Prodical [*in shocked and pained surprise*]. Me ?

Reiligan [*impatiently*]. You, yes, you ; you, you. Off to
the kitchen with you !

Canon [*warningly*]. Count, Count, speak more mildly like
a good man to another good man.

Reiligan [*ignoring the Monsignor*]. Go on an' don't stay to
argue — I'm orderin' you !

Prodical [*a gleam coming into his eyes*]. Y'are, are you ?

Canon [*smoothly*]. Not ordering, no, not ordering ; just
appealing to your generosity, Prodical.

Father Boheroe [*amused*]. Let the Bishop do with bread and
do without the plover.

Canon [*to Father Boheroe*]. Please, Father Boheroe, if you've
nothing constructive to say, say nothing.

Daniel [*from the door right*]. Let the Bishop peel his own
spuds !

Keelin [*from the door left — in a shout*]. Let the Bishop
pluck his own plover !

Canon [*angrily*]. Children, children, don't be acting the
goat ! St. Tremolo's ashamed of you ; St. Casabianca's ashamed of you ; I'm ashamed of you. [*To
the Prodical*] Mr. Carranaun, be sensible.

Prodical [*indignantly — to the Canon*]. Would you like to
dispel your stattus in order to pluck plovers an' peel
spuds !

Canon [*appealingly*]. It's for the Bishop, my son, for the Bishop. Peeling spuds for a Bishop, or plucking plovers for a Bishop, only adds to our stattuses, my dear man.

Prodical [*violently*]. I won't be wheedled ! [*He unties the strings of his apron.*] I won't do it ! [*He flings the apron at Foorawn.*] Let the lady put this on for a change. After an age of prayer, a spot of honest work'll do her soul good !

Canon [*almost putting an arm round the Prodical*]. My dear Protestant friend, this is a rare occasion ; only this once ; you will, won't you ?

Prodical [*yielding*]. Maybe this once, then.

Canon [*all smiles*]. My dear friend, thanks. [*To Daniel*] And you, too, Dan, come along and join us.

Daniel [*coming in hesitantly*]. Well, maybe, this once.

Canon. Grand. We must be a united family for this coming event. [*To Keelin*] You, too, daughter, come on in and join us.

Keelin [*as she goes, slamming the door behind her*]. I hope yous'll all be settled spiced in hell, soon, the whole of yous hungry, with flocks of plucked plovers yous can't catch flyin' round yous !

Canon [*undismayed*]. Never mind her, children. We mustn't get angry. A united family. Irish, too ; and the Irish aren't at their best when they're angry ; only when they're smiling ; smilin' through.
  [*The Canon has picked up Prodical's apron, and has begun to tie it back round Prodical's waist, as he lilts his little flattering ditty, in a half-nasal, semi-husky voice.*]

When Irish eyes are smilin',
Sure it's like a morn in spring ;
In the lilt of Irish laughter,
You can hear the angels sing.

[*Reiligan, Daniel, and the Prodical join in, rather
sheepishly, while Father Boheroe and Foorawn look on, and
listen, amused and a little scornful.*

When Irish hearts are happy,
All the world seems bright and gay,
When Irish eyes are smilin',
Sure, they steal your heart away !

[*During this singing the Codger has appeared at the
window and has gapingly listened to the chanting, a good
measure of scorn in his looking.   He carries in one hand
a saw and a hammer, and over one shoulder a scythe and a
hay-fork.   The blade of the scythe is heavily sheathed in
sacking so as to protect anyone from injury.*

Codger [*mockingly*]. A happy, holy family ! [*Flings the
hammer into the room*] There's your hammer. [*He
flings the saw in*] There's your saw. [*He flings the hay-
fork in*] There's your hay-fork. Take them up and
treat them kindly while your eyes are smiling.   The
scythe's me own.   Give me regards to your Bishop.
[*He turns away and goes slowly off down the path, and out
by the gate, singing :*]
Ah, bless'd be the day when I follow'd the plough,
An' the birds follow'd me with a peck and a bow,
Though I'm bending low now, an' I feel, ah so old,
Me heart is still young an' me spirit's still bold !

Canon [*as the gate clangs shut*]. That's the last of the old
ruffian, thank God.   Him and his songs !

Father Boheroe. I wish I could put into my prayers the

spirit he puts into his songs.   I'm afraid, Monsignor, God listens more eagerly to the songs of the Codger than He does to our best prayers.

Reiligan. I'm sorry at losin' the Codger, but he must be nearin' his end anyhow. [*To Prodical and Daniel — indicating saw, hammer, and hay-fork*] Take them things outa the way with yous, please.
   [*Prodical and Daniel pick them up, and go off carrying them out.*

Canon [*testily*]. Oh, let's get on with what we've to do. [*He looks at the list at the end of table.*] Gilded looking-glass, right ; rug and hot-water bottles, right. Oh, the wine isn't ticked off — has it come ?

Foorawn [*at door — calling into hall*]. Is the wine come yet ?

Prodical [*heard asking up the hall*]. Is the wine come yet ?

Voice [*farther on*]. No, wine isn't come yet.

Prodical [*calling back*]. No, wine isn't come yet.

Foorawn [*from the door to Canon*]. No, wine isn't come yet.
   [*Manus enters, morose and sullen, by the door where Foorawn is standing.   She backs a little way, and half extends her hands to him, then takes them slowly back. He passes by without apparent notice, and goes to the end of the table where the papers are.   He carries a thin ledger which he lays down on the table beside the papers. He is dressed as he was before, but now wears an old air-force, buttonless top-coat over his old shirt.   He wears the old hat still pulled down over his eyes.   The Canon eyes him coldly, but Reiligan greets him with forced geniality.*

Reiligan [*cordially*]. Well, Manus, me lad, everything all right ?

Manus. All serene.   Everything has come, including the wine.   You can all turn your minds to cheering.
[*He goes to the sideboard, fills out a generous glass of brandy, adding a splash of soda-water.*

Canon [*deprecatingly*].   That's the Bishop's brandy, Moanroe. I chose it myself for him.

Manus [*coolly*].   Did you ?   [*He lifts the glass*] To Manus Moanroe !   [*He drinks.*]   Ah, fine !   You've a good taste in brandy, Monsignor.   [*He returns to the table, and glances through a few pages of the ledger.*]   Everything, Count, is set down in best accountant's style.   This entertainment's going to cost you a pretty penny. Never mind — all for the glory of God's Bishop and the honour of Ballyoonagh.   Have a look at it, Count, and see if it's all right.

Reiligan.   No time now, Manus, oul' son ; we'll look over it when things have settled down.   Tomorrow, maybe.

Manus.   I won't be here tomorrow.   [*Goes to sideboard, fills out a glass of brandy again, and drinks it.*]   To me own Godspeed !   I'm leaving Ballyoonagh tonight — now.

Foorawn [*with a self-stifled catch in her voice*].   Oh, Manus !

Reiligan [*trying to disbelieve it*].   Nonsense !   You couldn't leave me — me right-hand man.   Look at the state you're in, an' you've no money.   [*He puts a hand affectionately on the shoulder of Manus*]   Your goin' would leave the stars over Ballyoonagh lonely.

Manus [*to Reiligan*].   I've enough money waiting for me ; don't worry.   Bar the Codger, you are the only man who ever told me there were stars over Ballyoonagh. I've never seen them meself. There's never been but one star in Ballyoonagh for me. I go now. [*He points to the ledger.*] There's the ledger made up to the last penny of today's accounting. [*He goes to the sideboard, and fills himself out another drink.*] A drink at the door! The Bishop won't grudge it to me. I like to do a thing thoroughly, if I do it at all.

Canon [*bitterly*]. Pity you weren't thorough enough to follow the way to the glory and honour of the priest-hood, the time you were at College, after the then Bishop had paid your fees. The time you slunk off, away from the College, and away from Ballyoonagh.

> [*There is a tense pause as Manus stands stiff, the glass half-way to his mouth. His eyes flash, but he shakes the anger off partly by a reckless shrug of his shoulders.*

Father Boheroe [*to Manus and to all*]. Those words are black against charity and truth, Manus. They are false to charity, and you must not weave them into a cold and dreary cape to drag your shoulders down.

Manus [*with a bitter laugh — drinking*]. To Manus Moanroe, the dead priest! [*Coldly — to the Canon*] I had more exciting times, in many places far away from Bally-oonagh. [*He tosses the glass into the fireplace.*] When I think of the Bishop who's coming, and look at the Monsignor who's here, I'm glad I escaped from the honour and glory of the priesthood!

> [*He goes towards the window.*

Foorawn [*anguished*]. Oh, Manus, Manus, don't be so bitter!

Manus [*without looking at her*]. Goodbye!

Reiligan [*as he goes*]. I'm sorry, very sorry, Manus.
  [*He goes out by the window, crosses the garden, opens the
  gate, and the clang of its shutting can be heard as he
  closes it, and goes out of sight.*

Canon [*with decision*]. A very good riddance !
  [*The telephone on the ledge beside the bureau rings, and
  Reiligan takes the call.*

Reiligan [*into the mouth-piece*]. Yes ? Oh, yes, Councillor.
  Lovely, is it ? It should be. Round towers, sham-
  rocks, an' wolf dogs all done to the life, huh ? Grand.
  Me and the Monsignor will be down in five minutes.
  Right. [*He replaces the receiver — to Canon*] The Coun-
  cillors are waitin' in the Parish Hall for us to top
  the Illuminated Address with our names. Secretary
  Mulvey says it's lovely. In a beautiful golden frame.
  The Bishop will be a proud man.

Canon [*briskly*]. We'll go now, Count.

Reiligan. Me car's outside.
                    [*They go out by the door on the right.*

Foorawn. Aren't you goin' to put your name on the
  address, Father Boheroe ?

Father Boheroe. I haven't been asked. You saw yourself,
  my dear : the Count and the Monsignor pretended to
  notice that I wasn't here. My name has been banished
  from among the wolf dogs, the shamrocks, and the
  round towers. [*He sits in a chair by the table, close to the
  image of St. Tremolo.*] Oh, Foorawn, I am something
  tired of it all.

Foorawn. Tired of what, Father ?

Father Boheroe. Of all the gilded foolishness claimed to
come so gleefully from God.

> [*He puts his arms on the table and wearily lays his head
> down between them. Foorawn pours some brandy into a
> glass, adds soda-water, and brings the drink to Father
> Boheroe.*

Foorawn [*touching his shoulder timidly, but affectionately*].
Drink this wee drop, Father, an' stiffen away your
weariness.

> [*He raises his head, looks at the glass for a few moments,
> hesitates, then takes the glass from her, and drinks the
> brandy.*

Father Boheroe. Thanks, Foorawn, agradh ; I needed it.
God help us, it's poor some of the things are that give
us courage to stand up, and go on.

Foorawn. It's so, Father, that you take too little, an'
Manus takes too much.

Father Boheroe. Ah, yes ; poor Manus ! Meeting with
him'll torment you no more. He's gone, and Ballyoonagh will be an empty place to you, now.

Foorawn [*firmly, but with twitching lip*]. I'm glad he's gone.
I hope I never set eyes on him ever again !

Father Boheroe [*after a pause*]. Not so long ago, Foorawn, he
was your lover, and you were his lass.

Foorawn [*fiercely*]. That's long ago, an' dead, an' dim, an'
gone for ever !

Father Boheroe. It was but yesterday to him ; and, if you
would only say truth, it was but yesterday to you.

Foorawn [*passionately*]. I have forgotten it ; I must forget it !

Father Boheroe. You have not forgotten it ; you can never forget it.

Foorawn [*appealingly*]. Oh, Father Boheroe, help me to persuade myself that I've forgotten it all. Help me ; pity me ; do not hinder me.

Father Boheroe. I am not able to help you, but I do not hinder you ; would not hinder you.

Foorawn. But you say things to remind me of what is all over, an' say nothing to help me to forget it all.

Father Boheroe. I cannot help you to forget what you can never forget yourself. You love Manus now as you loved him once. He is still an image bright in your eyes, deep in your heart. If you could change the image to the man, and hold him in your arms for a year and a day, the colours might dim, the light from it be less ; it would become a common man full of anxiety and fret, of sorrow today, of laughter to-morrow ; a life offending you, hurting you, even, at times ; but the common man would help you to laugh, too, help you to love when a child crept into your arms ; a love you may miss unto tears in the years that are to come.

Foorawn [*resentful, but moved*]. You talk curious, Father ; talk as if I had thrown me vow away, and had hidden meself in Manus Moanroe's arms !

Father Boheroe. You haven't thrown your vow away ; you would be afraid to do it ; but you are in his arms, all the same.

Foorawn [*vehemently*]. I am not ! The Monsignor, when he was Canon, has praised me often an' often ; an' the very Bishop comin' here has praised me once.

Father Boheroe. I can hear the two worldly and ambitious men speaking. God help us ! You've only to read his pastorals to see that Bill Mullarkey with a bishop's robe on his back, a bishop's ring on his finger, and a bishop's mitre on his head, is Bill Mullarkey still. [*A pause.*] Ask him to release you from your foolish vows, Foorawn. Be brave.

Foorawn [*shocked*]. Oh, Father Boheroe ! Don't say such things. You know the Bishop would never consent to release me from my vow. I daren't ask him.

Father Boheroe. Then ask God, my daughter.

Foorawn. Ask God ? How could I ever possibly know that God wouldn't be angry with me for breaking my vow ?

Father Boheroe. How did you know that God was pleased when you took it ?

Foorawn. The Canon told me, the Bishop told me.

Father Boheroe. Oh, yes, the Bishop and the Canon. I forgot them. They hear everything that God says.

Foorawn [*with uneasy indignation*]. What kind of a priest are you, sayin' such things ! Muddlin' a young girl's mind against turnin' her face to God, an' turnin' her back on the world, the flesh, an' the devil.

Father Boheroe. Ah, Foorawn, it is easy to turn one's back on things, but it is better and braver to face them. I shall never turn my back on a beautiful world, nor on the beautiful flesh of humanity, asparkle with vigour, intelligence, and health ; and as for the devil, what we often declare to be the devil is but truth who has at last mustered the courage to speak it.

Foorawn. You aren't much help to God. You seem to feel for none. I've noticed you with the Prodical, ignoring his needs. Once, he seemed to be knocking at the door of our church, and you never tried to open it to him.

Father Boheroe [*rising to his feet — a little impatiently*]. Oh, don't worry about the Prodical — he's safer than you or I.

Foorawn [*shocked*]. Safer than us !

Father Boheroe [*moving towards the window*]. He has helped to build hospitals where the sick shelter, homes where we live, churches even where we worship ; he serves God as a mason better than I do in my priesthood, or you in your chastity.

Foorawn [*with some sarcasm*]. A great fella indeed ! Are you goin' to watch the Bishop's Bonfire ?

Father Boheroe. I had forgotten the bonfire. No, Foorawn, my road goes in an opposite direction, where, though there be no cedars, at least, I shall walk under the stars. Come with me, and, maybe, we shall find something to say that will encourage us to go more firmly through the woe of life.

Foorawn [*in shocked amazement*]. An' supposin' someone saw us walkin' together on a lonely road in the dead of the night-time ?

Father Boheroe [*with mock seriousness*]. That would be terrible, Foorawn ! We are dead people, and must learn to lie circumspectly in our shrouds.

Foorawn [*reproachfully*]. You try to mock me, but should

mock yourself. You have tried, and failed, Father.
You have failed poor Keelin.

Father Boheroe. I did my best.

Foorawn [*bitterly*]. You have given no help to me, Father.

Father Boheroe. I did my best.

Foorawn. Or to Manus either.

Father Boheroe. Or to him, though God knows I'd dearly
like to help you both. [*With some scorn*] Here in the
room, Foorawn, you have two saints, and neither the
one here [*he indicates St. Tremolo*], nor that one there [*he
indicates St. Casabianca*], opened a gob, or blew the
Bookineeno, to say a word, or give a sign of help.
When we have problems, Foorawn, ourselves are the
saints to solve them. Our weakness—and our strength.

Foorawn [*opening the door on right to go out*]. You frighten
me sometimes, Father. I'm going. Good night, Father
Boheroe.

Father Boheroe [*appealingly*]. Foorawn, Foorawn, don't be
too hard on a poor priest unable to work a miracle !

Foorawn [*coldly as she goes out, and shuts the door behind her*].
Good-bye, Father.
   [*Father Boheroe goes out into the garden as the Prodical
   comes in by the door on left.*

Prodical [*out to Father Boheroe*]. Off to watch the Bishop's
Bonfire, Father ?

Father Boheroe [*calling back — angrily*]. Oh, to hell with
the Bishop's Bonfire !

Prodical [*surprised and shocked*]. Oh ? What ails him, now, I wonder ? A lot of the glamour's goin' into gloom.
[*He peers out into the garden, then puts some fingers into his mouth, and gives a long, shrill whistle. After a few moments, the Codger appears before him.*

Codger. I'm here, me son ; waitin'. [*He turns to gaze into the distance.*] Looka all the twinklin' lights from the lanterns carried be them comin' up the valleys and down the hills to meet the Bishop an' watch his Bonfire blazin' ! Twinklin' lights. Man-made stars risin' a little from the earth, but never soarin' too high.

Prodical [*fussily*]. Let's not bother now about twinklin' lights or blazin' bonfires. You know the ordeal in front of us. What we have to do is to snatch the bottle I hid under the Bookineeno boyo ; for without it, we'll be destitute.

Codger. It was a maniacal thing to do ! Are they all gone to see the Bonfire ?

Prodical. Yes, though I'm not sure about Foorawn. I seen her puttin' on her cloak, takin' it off, an' puttin' it on again. [*He comes in, creeps close to the Codger, and whispers :*] Listen — we'll do it in darkness to confuse him. Hum one of your tunes as if we were only casually reconnoiterin'.

Codger [*turning out the light*]. A good idea. I'll lift, you snatch. [*He hums a bar or two of 'My Bonnie' — suddenly*] Now ! [*He lifts the statue with a swift movement, and the Prodical snatches the bottle away from under it. At the same moment the Bookineeno gives out a long, wailing, trumpet-like bar of sound. Codger dumps the statue back on to the table swiftly. Making for the window*]

Saint Michael, head of the fightin' angels, keep him off me !

[*The Prodical and the Codger, with the bottle of whiskey, rush out, and disappear around by the ash tree.*

[*A pause. When the running sound of the footsteps has gone from a hearing, and the wail of the Bookineeno has died down, Manus is seen outside in the garden. A cloth cap is now on his head, the peak pulled well down over his eyes. He takes the lantern from the top of the bricks, and, carrying it with him, enters the room by the window. He stands to listen for a few moments, pulling his cap down further over his eyes, then goes to the bureau, over which the votive-light burns, and the Saint stands. He takes a steel chisel from a pocket, and prises a drawer open, and takes a bundle of notes from it. He looks at the bundle to read an inscription on a slip attached to it.*

Manus [*reading — mockingly*]. Pro Deo et ecclesia. For God and Church. For Manus and his doxies now. She forgot to write that down. Wants me to be barren as herself. [*He catches sight of the gun as he puts the notes into a pocket. He takes the gun from its holster, and slips it into another one.*] Saint Casabianca, you're a bad boy : over the money and beside the gun. The lack of a gun and the loss of the money will make you a little more like a saint. [*He wheels to face the door on right as Foorawn enters, switching on the light as she comes into the room. The two stare at each other speechless for a few moments. Recovering himself*] Oh, what a surprise !

Foorawn [*coldly*]. What are you doing there ?

Manus [*pouring out a glass of brandy and offering it to her*]. Have a drink, dear ; it'll make you warmer in your voice.

Foorawn. I don't drink.

Manus. More for meself. [*He drinks.*] Forgot. You don't drink, smoke, dance, go to a cinema, read bad books, or ever swear. You are a real puritanical bitch, but [*he pauses a moment*] you are a very beautiful one.

Foorawn [*as coldly as before*]. What are you doin' there, Moanroe ?

Manus. Damn it, can't you see, Foorawn, daughter of Reiligan ? I'm stealing a little from a lot stolen from many.

Foorawn. It wasn't stolen ; it is money saved from the reward given for honest work done.

Manus [*hilariously*]. For work done ! For setting up an appearance of sanctity, you mean, before a front of fraud !

Foorawn [*angry now*]. Fraud ! What fraud, you gaspin' throw-away from the Church eternal ! What fraud, you rusty drunkard ! What fraud ?

Manus [*quietly and firmly*]. The fraud of clericals forbidding drink in the dance halls, though here, in Ballyoonagh, drinkers from Reiligan's tavern go to the dance hall to dance, and dancers from Reiligan's dance hall go to Reiligan's tavern to drink ; the fraud of Reiligan's town stores where there's nothing in spirit or manner to show that life's more than meat, and the body than raiment ; the fraud of his mean meadows where his bunchy cattle low their woe to God for want of grass ; the fraud of his shirt factory where girls work but to earn enough to leave the land, and where there's more melody in the heart of a machine than in the heart of its minder.

Foorawn [*more calmly than before*]. Having said your say, lustiest fraud of them all, leave the money back where you got it, an' go.

Manus [*mildly*]. You ask too much, my love.

Foorawn [*appealingly*]. Manus, what you do is sacrilege.

Manus. I'm a bad one, sweetheart, but you are wrong, my sombre musk rose — the notes haven't been consecrated.

Foorawn. It's you are wrong ; the drawer was blessed top, bottom, and on either side by the Canon himself.

Manus. Ah, how readily the Canon would bless any place where money lay ! For him the cosy parlour and the glass of grog ; for him no part in the rainfall at morning and the dew-fall at night. But blessing is different from consecration. If the Canon complains, tell him Manus took the notes from their sacred hiding-place as David took the shewbread from the holy altar.
   [*He moves towards the window. She rushes over and grabs hold of him.*

Foorawn [*struggling with him*]. Give them back, and go your wicked way !

Manus [*flinging her from him*]. Oh, let me go, you mournful, empty shell of womanhood !

Foorawn [*running to the telephone, and whipping up the receiver*]. I'll get the police ! I'll watch you hauled to jail ; I'll have you finished in this whole district, in this whole land !

Manus. So that's your love and that's your charity, Foorawn's love and Foorawn's charity, you sounding cymbal, you junk of tinkling brass ! [*Wildly, a deep menace in his voice, taking the gun from his pocket*] Get away from that ! D'ye hear ? Drop that phone, you bitch !

Foorawn [*wildly and passionately*]. I'll settle you for ever, you spoiled priest ! [*He fires at her. She drops the telephone, seems stunned for a second. Then she goes to the table-end where the ledger and the papers are and, pressing a hand to her side, sinks down on the chair that stands there. As she staggers to the chair*] You ruffian ! Oh, Manus, darling, I think I'm dying. [*She takes up a pen, and writes some words on a paper lying on the table.*] Give me the gun — quick — before I go ! The gun !
  [*He offers it to her in a dazed way, she takes it in a hand, Manus staring at her, sinking forward over the table.*

Manus [*very low*]. Go on, shoot me, before the strength of hate leaks away from your weakening white arm.

Foorawn [*softly — half to herself, half to Manus*]. Oh, Manus, I loved you once. I love you now. I love——
  [*She dies. He switches off the light, giving the room dark-ness, showing more plainly the red glare in the sky from the Bishop's Bonfire. He crosses over and replaces the receiver on the telephone ; comes back to where she sits on the chair, her head and shoulders resting on the table, her arm and the hand, holding the gun, stretched out, half encircling the statue of St. Tremolo. He takes up the paper on which she had written, takes it up slowly, and looks over it.*

Manus [*reading slowly and softly — in stifled anguish*]. 'I can bear this life no longer. Good-bye all. Foorawn.' [*He slowly places the paper back on the table.*] Oh, my poor Foorawn ! My sombre musk rose ; my withered musk rose now !

[*The sound of distant cheering is heard as Manus lifts the lantern and goes towards the window. Before he reaches it, the sound of the Codger's voice is heard speaking to the Prodical in the garden. Manus goes softly to the side of the window, pressing himself against the curtain, and holding the lantern so that its light cannot be seen by anyone outside.*]

Codger. There goes the Bishop's Bonfire blazing high ! An' the cheerin' — the Bishop has come to Bally-oonagh !

Prodical [*irritably*]. Never mind the Bishop or the Bishop's Bonfire ! I'm your friend, not the Bishop. With our bottle of wine an' bottle of whiskey, and a tasty snack in my little shanty, we'll keep the night aglow by a tait-a-tait talk about the woes an' wonders of the world. Go on with your singin', Codger, an' shorten the road before us. A Count now, begod !

Codger. He wouldn't like it if he knew we were takin' a short cut through his lovely garden. Window open, an' all dark. [*Exclaiming*] Begod, the lantern's gone from the top of the bricks !

Prodical [*impatiently*]. Never mind about the lantern, the Bishop, or the Bishop's Bonfire or the Bookineeno boys now — them's trivial things ! I'm your friend now, amn't I ? am I, or amn't I ? We have to think of what we have to do with the woes an' wonders of the world. Come on, an' go on with the song you were singin', for I'm in a mournful mood.

Codger. We're all in a mournful mood, merrily mournful all. [*Singing :*]

Last night as I lay on me pilla, last night as I lay on
    me bed
Last night as I lay on me pilla, I dreamt me dear
    Bonnie was dead.

Codger
Prodical } [*singing together*] :

Bring back, bring back, bring back my Bonnie to me,
    to me,
Bring back, bring back, O bring back my Bonnie to
    me.

  [*When the song has died away, Manus takes up the lantern,
  goes out into the garden, and replaces it on top of the
  bricks ; then he comes back to the window, closes it, and
  goes slouching away out of sight ; while the Bishop's
  Bonfire flames higher and more brightly, and the cheers
  are heard a little more clearly.*

END OF THE PLAY

THE ROSE THAT IS FRESH

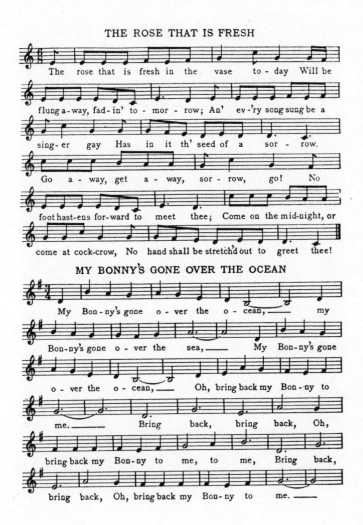

The rose that is fresh in the vase to-day Will be flung a-way, fad-in' to-mor-row; An' ev-'ry song sung be a sing-er gay Has in it th' seed of a sor-row. Go a-way, get a-way, sor-row, go! No foot hast-ens for-ward to meet thee; Come on the mid-night, or come at cock-crow, No hand shall be stretch'd out to greet thee!

MY BONNY'S GONE OVER THE OCEAN

My Bon-ny's gone o-ver the o-cean, ____ my Bon-ny's gone o-ver the sea, ____ My Bon-ny's gone o-ver the o-cean, ____ Oh, bring back my Bon-ny to me. ____ Bring back, bring back, Oh, bring back my Bon-ny to me, to me, Bring back, bring back, Oh, bring back my Bon-ny to me. ____

AH, BLEST BE THE DAY

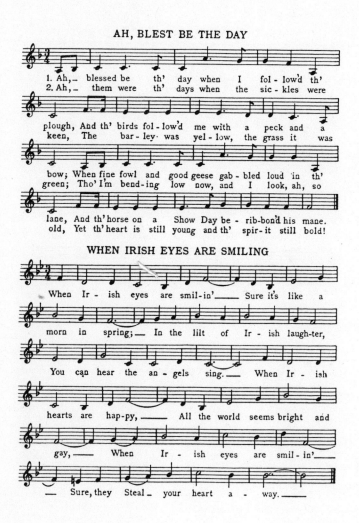

1. Ah,— blessed be th' day when I fol-low'd th'
2. Ah,— them were th' days when the sic-kles were

plough, And th' birds fol-low'd me with a peck and a
keen, The bar-ley was yel-low, the grass it was

bow; When fine fowl and good geese gab-bled loud in th'
green; Tho' I'm bend-ing low now, and I look, ah, so

lane, And th' horse on a Show Day be-rib-bon'd his mane.
old, Yet th' heart is still young and th' spir-it still bold!

WHEN IRISH EYES ARE SMILING

When Ir-ish eyes are smil-in'___ Sure it's like a

morn in spring;___ In the lilt of Ir-ish laugh-ter,

You can hear the an-gels sing.___ When Ir-ish

hearts are hap-py, ___ All the world seems bright and

gay, ___ When Ir-ish eyes are smil-in'___

___ Sure, they Steal_ your heart a-way.___

AH, THEM WERE THE GOLDEN DAYS

Ah,   them were th' gold - en days with an
Oh,   where is th' laugh - ter rich   of

arm a-round a waist___ When ev-'ry-thing shone so shy an'
chil-dren mad at play.___ Gone, too, is the lov - er an' his

gay;___   When   a   man   had heart to toss th'
lass ___   from   all   the haw - thorns frag - rance

girls   as well   as time   to   toss th' hay— Ah
in   the month of June   or month of May. Ah,

them were th' days when life had some-thing fine to say!___
where is the time when life had some-thing fine to say!___

THE END